AVATAR

AVATAR

A CONFIDENTIAL REPORT ON THE BIOLOGICAL AND SOCIAL HISTORY OF PANDORA

MARIA WILHELM & DIRK MATHISON

HarperCollins*Publishers*

HarperCollins*Publishers*
77-85 Fulham Palace Road,
Hammersmith, London W6 8JB

www.harpercollins.co.uk

First published in the USA in 2009 by !t Books, an imprint of
HarperCollins*Publishers*

This edition 2009

10 9 8 7 6 5 4 3 2

A catalogue record of this book is available from the British Library

ISBN 978-0-00-734244-0

Designed by Aline C. Pace

Printed and bound by Butler Tanner & Dennis, Frome, Somerset

"THERE ARE MANY DANGERS ON PANDORA, AND ONE
OF THE SUBTLEST IS THAT YOU MAY COME TO LOVE
IT TOO MUCH."

—DR. GRACE AUGUSTINE

A SURVIVAL HANDBOOK

FELLOW TERRANS

The armies of greed lay waste to the Earth and all its creatures. In our hunger for energy—for more and more—we've devastated our planet. We're neck-deep in festering industrial muck, in a trash heap of ever-expanding waste and decay. Overpopulation, overdevelopment, nuclear terrorism, environmental warfare, radiation leakage from power plants and waste dumps, toxic runoff, air pollution, deforestation, global warming, ozone depletion, loss of biodiversity through extinction . . . our once blue-green and beauteous Earth is now a terminal cesspool—an oozing wound cut deep into the face of the universe. Dollar for dollar, we've bought our extinction.

So who am I? I'm a neighbor, a friend, the enemy. I am anonymous. I am invisible. I am everywhere. I shuffle past you in a dense crowd, shoulder to jammed shoulder, unwashed because of the water shortages, stinking and sickly-looking from the bankrupt diet of cheap carbohydrates and synthetic proteins that are all we have left. Like you, I'm trapped in a rat warren of dusty gray concrete; tracked by the omnivorous, all-powerful net; sucking in sulfurous air; badly outnumbered; mostly numbed. I'm scarred, scared, hunted, and all too human.

What energy I have left is fueled by rage—by the incendiary and explosive rage of a dying, decimated planet!

I look around at the garbage-strewn, high-tech squalor here and see in the murky distance that much better place—pristine Pandora, opalescent in the velvet darkness. Our hope and salvation lies in her fertile and gracious beauty; in the panoply of her brilliantly colored flora and fauna; in her fierce and bountiful mother-love.

But the insidious greed of the megacorporations has breached planetary boundaries. It's spreading over Pandora like a fast-growing fungus, wreaking destruction of a deliberate force and calculated magnitude not seen since the demolition of our once-proud Earth.

Know that you are in extreme danger. The document you have received is critical to the survival of Pandora and to your survival here on Earth. It's composed of purloined notes, stolen files smuggled off the moon, hijacked data mined in ways I can't reveal and by people—growing and courageous—who have risked their lives to disseminate these truths.

There is no guarantee of the accuracy of this information. But either way, they don't want you to have it. They want to you to stay stunned and stupid, in bovinelike complacency, chewing carefully manufactured lies. Use extreme caution. They are watching, hidden in the tall grass of the ever-present web, waiting. . . .

So organize! Enlist others! Propagate the hard and painful truth! Stop the spread of the lethal corporate poison!

Think of the hope of Pandora and of the Na'vi. They have little or no technology. Yet it is we who scrape for survival while they feast on the bounty of a thriving land, teeming with life. Can the knowledge of a sacred world steer us away from a terrible fate? Perhaps not. We know the truth. It may be the only hope for Pandora and for our sad and battered Earth. Ask yourself: If we can't save Pandora, how can we save ourselves?

Join us and fight. Fight for Pandora! Fight for Earth! Fight for your own survival!

This is a survival handbook—survival both for ourselves as individuals and for our beloved planet. The data I and others have complied at mortal risk will help detoxify our violated, bone-brittle land, will help purify our water, and, yes, will help fight back the pulverizing, carnivorous greed that keeps us dumb and in servitude.

Make no mistake—our explicit goal is to dismantle the RDA. And, by doing so, to save Pandora and Earth itself. Laboring off-net, we have collected highly valuable field notes on Pandoran astrobotany, geology, anthropology, paleontology, biology—sciences spanning millennia and born from the curiosity and wonder and awe that made us who we once were. That made us human. The information presented both informs and warns. Use it. It's all you've got and much more than they let you have.

There is a richness on Pandora much greater than any mineral. Her bounty will save us. The simple dakteron, for example, an exotic Pandoran flower with remarkable medicinal powers, can eradicate the global scourge of River Blindness. The octoshroom, a fast-growing radio-tropic fungus, absorbs various soil poisons and can cleanse the Nevada Toxic Flats. *Teylu*, a self-replicating grub that is a source of protein more complete and more nourishing than our vanishing phytoplanktons, is critical to sustaining life (our now diminished life . . .) as we've come to know it.

There are no national parks left, as you know, only file-cabinet, lock-box housing, and protein farms. The great Yosemite, with its towering granite domes and spectacular peaks, is an upscale condo development. The 64-meter Grizzly Giant, a sequoia that stood in defiance for thousands of years, was splintered for fuel long ago. That thundering cascade of once-pure mountain water—the 739-meter Yosemite Falls—is now a thin and sickly drizzle. Most oceanfront property is used for mariculture; the only food source efficient enough to feed everyone these days is spirulina. It's amazing the things you can do with algal protein concentrate if you know your spices.

I'm pretty much confined to my cube, if you care. I look like you—crepuscular, an endomorph, a sapsucker. But where there was no point or purpose there's now the "cause." Surprised and baffled, I tumbled into love. The defining xenobotanist, the Charles Darwin of Pandora, Dr. Grace Augustine, became my leader and my light. I am doing this for her—always for her.

Through her inspiration, Pandora awakened in me. I began to dream. Bigger dreams than my standard four-by-six, unlimited and awake to that place far beyond our parched yellow sky, in the blue-black causeway of Earth above.

I became lured by a magic and a mystery out there, by hope and belief in an informed spirit woven through Pandora that is the author and origin of the vital interconnectedness of all its living things. It's not a myth. Or a belief born of sham faith. On Pandora there is only one greater entity. She spreads beneath the ground in a complex root system like the

neural pathways in the human brain, with every tree being a single brain cell, or dendrite. And all the roots comingling . . . those are the synapses. One vast sentience, covering all the land.

The Na'vi call her Eywa. Is she intelligent, this Eywa? Sort of. But she's more like a kind of bio-Internet. She's a memory-keeper, a collective consciousness, a precisely calibrated scale. She logs the thoughts and feelings of everything that thinks and feels. Her function is to bring balance to the systemic whole, one that is perfectly interdependent, biodiverse, self-regulating, and unified.

But more than a network, she has a will. An ego. She guides, she shapes, she protects. Sometimes she sacrifices something she loves for the greater good. Eywa does not take sides; Eywa will not necessarily save you. Her role is to protect all life, and the balance of life. She is, quite literally, Mother Nature.

"Mother," I sometimes cry out. We are lost—through callous greed, through inattention, though our pervasive, intransigent, and determined stupidity.

But they like us that way, of course. Dumb. In half-sleep. Rewarded for surrender.

Don't be.

Know your enemy, know the lawless bastards who've enslaved the sun and dictate the day and the darkness; who, Santa-like, decide if you've been bad or good; who sell you a permanent and insatiable jones via a nutrient-free foodpac.

It's the aforementioned RDA, the Resources Development Administration, your friendly neighborhood supercorp, which has the rights, in perpetuity, to pillage and plunder outer space . . . and inner. The RDA started as a garage band, a benign lil' twenty-first-century Silicon Valley start-up funded on borrowed dollars from friends and family. Today, it's the largest single commercially directed organization in the universe, with a monopoly on all products shipped, derived, or developed from mineral-rich Pandora, that delicate moon in balletic orbit around the gas giant planet, Polyphemus.

You may not know the background. Unfettered both by regulations and by gravity, the RDA started by taking control of the sky. Hundreds of orbiting factories on the Earth's moon, Mars, and the solar system's asteroid belt were in operation just a few decades after it was formed. Those factories started raining toxins down on Earth from above. Yes, a continual downpour of poisons . . . on you.

Feeding the ever-expanding energy maw, the "Consortium," as it's less-than-affectionately called, expanded its reach with the discovery on Pandora of unobtanium—one of the most sought after, valuable, and profitable materials ever found, with a value exponentially more than that of gold.

Unique to Pandora, unobtanium, is a rare-earth compound and "high-temperature" superconductor. The room-temperature superconductor has been the "snark" of modern materials science—that long-coveted property that transmits electricity with zero resistance, but at room temperature and above, unlike the liquid helium–cooled super-conductors of human science. Unobtanium has become the backbone of Earth's economy. From extraction to distribution, the RDA controls it all.

The RDA makes money, as you know. Lots of money for lots of people. It has millions of shareholders and is now the oldest and most profitable of the quasi-governmental administrative entities (QGAEs). Like a fast-growing virus, it has insinuated itself into every aspect of our lives. That is, if how we exist and subsist down here constitutes "living."

But I feel a stirring hope in the permanent dusk of our time on earth. I close my eyes and imagine streamers and whorls of shredded cloud swirling around mountains that float—yes, float—in a turquoise sky. Cu-mulus, stratus, cirrus, and nimbus of hard rock, some more than sixteen kilometers across, hovering hundreds of meters above the ground. And waterfalls originating on mesa tops and traversing sheer cliffs like a cas-cade of jewels, then exploding into spray on the craggy bottoms in gey-sers . . . but upside down.

Twinkling like tiny flecks of ash on the wind are what look like birds, batlike flying creatures of various sizes. Some lushly colored, they appear as streaks of deep crimson cutting through crystal. Far below, on Pando-

ra's vast and verdant plains, a kaleidoscopic array of sturmbeest—tens of thousands of them—begin a plodding migration, their hoofbeats like drums.

Interwoven, I hear the meditative drone of a Na'vi song, gathering the clan, urging them home.

And then I see our scarred Earth, renewed and revived. The oceans returned to blue, a world washed clean and begun again. Like it once was. I can't help but wonder if Eywa called out to us, at risk to herself, so that she might save Earth.

1 ASTRONOMY AND GEOLOGY

At a distance of 4.37 light-years from Earth, the Alpha Centauri system is our nearest stellar neighbor. Although it appears as a single star, it is actually a trinary system that consists of two sunlike stars, Alpha Centauri A, Alpha Centauri B, and a red dwarf, Alpha Centauri C. Its largest member, Alpha Centauri A (or ACA to astronomers), serves as the sun for Pandora, a large moon that orbits the planet Polyphemus.

Pandora's proximity to Polyphemus and the other two closest moons produce tidal heating that helps increase rapid continental drift. This creates intense vulcanism and fractures large continental landmasses, moderating the moon's weather. The unique substance "unobtanium" has helped create a myriad of remarkable geological formations through its superconducting magnetic properties. These include the famous Hallelujah Mountains and the Stone Arches. Despite Pandora's alien landscape, there are Earth-like valleys, mountaintops, beaches, and lakes. Its unmarred beauty has sparked the imagination of Terrans everywhere.

The discovery and subsequent exploration of the Alpha Centauri system is one of the great achievements in science. But it is unobtanium that brought humans to Pandora. And, despite the enormous danger, it is why the RDA and its colonists remain there today.

PANDORA

LOCATION: A moon of Polyphemus, a gas giant planet orbiting the star Alpha Centauri A, roughly 4.4 light-years from Earth

ENVIRONMENT: Earth-like, but humans cannot breathe its air without an exopack

INHABITANTS: Na'vi, a highly intelligent humanoid race with a Neolithic society

RESOURCES: The only known source of unobtanium, a superconductor vital to Earth's economy

Although Pandora is a satellite of Polyphemus, it has much more in common with Earth than with our moon. Similar in size, atmosphere, and appearance, it has continents and islands surrounded by seas of a familiar blue hue. Clouds range in color from fluffy white to towering dark thunderheads. The landforms have mountains, valleys, plains, lakes, and rivers. Plant life is everywhere; forests and meadows cover much of the land, and rafts of floating seaweed dot the oceans. Vast herds of grazing animals roam the open prairie and huge flying creatures fill the skies.

Much of the plant life often contains chemical compounds that render it unfit for human consumption. Many of the species have poisonous thorns or pods that burst and spray acid sap. The animal life is also dangerous to humans. Thickly armored hammerheads are unstoppable with standard-issue assault rifles. Flying *ikran*, or "banshees," swoop down to snatch the unwary. Many smaller animals and insects, like the stingbat and hellfire wasp, have extremely potent venom. The native inhabitants are fierce warriors, and humans underestimate Na'vi capabilities at their own peril.

Yet Pandora has a beauty unsurpassed by anything on Earth. In the Pandoran night, every living thing blazes with phosphorescent rainbow hues—a flashing, flickering phantasmagoria of images that can quickly hypnotize a newcomer. On a spiritual level, it is believed there is a strange harmony that pervades all Pandoran life. The few humans who have embraced it say they experience a peace they have never known before.

The mysterious beauty of Pandora and knowledge of its sentient creatures have sparked the imagination of billions on Earth.

DISCOVERY

When astronomers turned a powerful space-based telescope toward the Alpha Centauri system and one of its planets, Polyphemus, they were stunned to find a moon that had an atmosphere with the spectro-scopic signature of free oxygen, in a concentration almost equal to Earth's.

Given the presence of oxygen, scientists believed that the moon could harbor life. Even more intriguing was the splitting of spectrographic lines that indicated the presence of intense magnetic fields, far stronger than any known outside of a star's interior.

This spurred the construction of even larger space telescopes. They revealed Pandora to be a verdant Earth-like world in the star system nearest to our own.

A subsequent unmanned mission led to the discovery of a world teeming with plants, animals, and geological oddities.

The research craft also discovered the source of the intense magnetic fields, a substance that had the remarkable property of high-temperature superconductivity.

It was this substance, later named unobtanium, that made it financially feasible to launch the manned exploration of Pandora. But it was the image of the Na'vi that empowered the world to come together to embrace the first manned mission to another star system.

PHYSICAL CHARACTERISTICS					
World	Diameter (kilometers)	Mass	Surface Gravity	Atmospheric Density	Surface Pressure
Earth	1275.27	1	1	1	1
Pandora	11447	0.72	0.8	1.2	1.1

GEOLOGY

Enormous magnetic storms caused by interactions with Polyphemus's magnetic field. Deadly animals. Toxic atmosphere. Unsurpassed beauty and spiritual harmony.

Pandora's physical construction resembles Earth's: a liquid iron core, a plastic mantle, and a semirigid crust. Like Earth, it has two internal heat sources: the disintegration of radioactive isotopes, and energy from the gravitational collapse of its initial formation. But there is an additional and much larger energy input from tidal forces; the nearest inner and outer moons pull on it in contest with Polyphemus.

This excess of energy drives continental drift at a much faster rate than on Earth, causing the tectonic plates to fracture more extensively because of the increased stress. This explains the lack of large continents on Pandora, as well as its vulcanism and geothermal activity.

Though Pandora's land-to-water ratio is greater than Earth's, the land is broken up into a larger number of smaller continents, creating more coastline and fewer inland regions than on Earth. The moderating influence of the proximity of the continental interiors to the oceans reduces extremes in temperature. Polar ice caps comparable to Earth's exist, but because there are no landmasses in the polar areas, the Pandoran ice caps are currently free-floating.

Pandora is more volcanically active than Earth. There are vents both on the land and under the oceans. Many of the mountains and other surface features are of recent volcanic origin. Numerous hot springs and geysers dot the landscape, and there are several rivers that are almost boiling at the place where they erupt from underground aquifers.

MAGNETIC FIELDS

Pandora possesses a liquid iron core, with circulating currents that produce a dipole field similar in structure to the Earth's, but the presence of unobtanium deposits deep below the surface magnifies its strength hundreds of times. This enhanced field shields the surface from cosmic rays or material ejected from Alpha Centauri A, but unlike Earth, these intense magnetic fields are not as uniform, and concentrated unobtanium deposits produce localized distortions to the worldwide field that can act as magnetic funnels. These anomalies can channel incoming particles ejected from the sun to the moon's surface. Any life-form unlucky enough to be caught in one of these

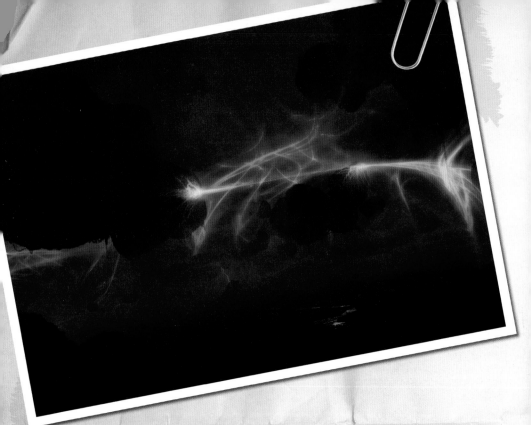

areas during a stellar flare event or CME (Coronal Mass Ejection) will be quickly irradiated with a lethal dose. Depending on the type and amount of radiation, death can occur instantly as brain tissue is ionized and effectively "shorts out," or be delayed for agonizing days or weeks as the tissue slowly necrotizes.

Pandora's global field also interacts with Polyphemus's much more extensive one. This can divert radiation trapped in the planet's magnetic field to the moon's surface—also with unpleasant results. Additionally, the configuration of these two fields produces a "magnetic flux tube" that links the polar areas of the planet and satellite with an electrical current flow of millions of amperes. This causes a gigantic increase in electrical activity on both bodies, with massive auroral storms and other electromagnetic phenomena.

ATMOSPHERE

Pandora is not Earth, and its paradise is deceiving. The nitrogen-oxygen atmosphere is 20 percent denser than our own. It contains so much carbon dioxide (more than 18 percent) that humans who breathe it directly will rapidly lose consciousness and die. Another gas, hydrogen sulfide, is spewed out by pervasive vulcanism, and is toxic in concentrations far less than 1 percent. It must be removed by the exopack's mask along with the CO_2. The heavy gas xenon comprises about 5.5 percent of Pandora's atmosphere, and is responsible for much of the increased air density. Although Pandora's air is denser than Earth's, the sea level pressure is about 10 percent less, in part because the moon's gravity is only 80 percent of Earth's.

AMP Suit

FUNCTION: Ambulatory weapons platform for military and civilian operations in hostile and toxic environments

OFFICIAL NAME: MK-6 Amplified Mobility Platform

NA'VI NAME: "Shield that walks" or "Not-demon walking"

SIZE AND WEIGHT: 4 meters in height, 1.83 meters wide

WEAPONRY: Shoulder-slung and detachable GAU-90 30-millimeter cannon. Belt-fed ammo runs through feed chute. Optional flame thrower, slashing blade.

The Amplified Mobility Platform (or "AMP Suit") is a refinement of a military exoskeleton device first used on Earth in the early twenty-first century and refined during wars over the decades. Sealed models for toxic environments were developed and, with the colonization of the moon and Mars, pressurized versions with full life-support systems were employed in great numbers.

The AMP Suit is a powerful all-terrain ground combat unit designed for use by infantry. It can survive the most hostile foe, be it alien or human, and cut a swath through difficult landscapes and strong enemy positions. Its enclosed cab and "BIBS" (Built-in-Breathing system) also allows RDA personnel to perform civilian and military duties in a variety of toxic atmospheres.

Although an operator can learn to adequately manipulate the unit in combat conditions with less than two months of training, it takes months longer to master the transition from a supine to an upright position. However, with the gyroscope and the operator's deft control, very few AMP Suits topple. Its auto balance technology automatically compensates for shifts in the AMP Suit's center of gravity, whether it is used for standing, walking, or lifting heavy loads.

If the operator has been injured or killed, the AMP Suit has an unmanned "walk-back" capability on battery power. This feature was developed to protect the significant capital investment made in each suit.

Not designed for Pandora, but suit is effective protection from toxic plants, swarms of stinging, aggressive insects, and other biting creatures.

EVEN WITH GYROS AND STABILITY CHIPS, IT'S EASIER TO KNOCK DOWN THAN THEY LET ON. A LENGTH OF WIRE CABLE, PROPERLY PLACED, DOES THE TRICK. CANNON'S AMMO FEED LINE HAS BEEN KNOWN TO JAM.

EXOPACK

Developed from civilian rebreather technology, the exopack is a lightweight atmosphere filtration system that allows humans to survive on Pandora with minimum equipment.

Pandora's atmosphere would be easily breathable—if it wasn't contaminated by a pungent mixture of carbon dioxide, xenon, and hydrogen sulfide. The additional gases cause a variety of unpleasant reactions, including choking and burning of mucous membranes, followed by unconsciousness within twenty seconds and death within four minutes.

Nevertheless, the partial pressure of oxygen in the Pandoran atmosphere is similar to that of Earth's atmosphere. In order to breathe, it is only necessary to filter out the toxic components.

The filters will function for two weeks before accumulated soot clogs the filter pores. The filter pads can be regenerated by gentle washing with running water and will last indefinitely with proper care.

A polymer static rim around the exopack mask ensures a light, tight seal around the face.

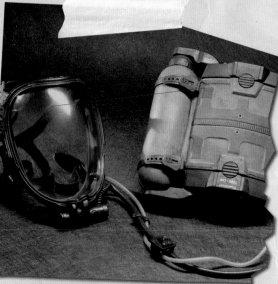

READ CAREFULLY— WON'T BE LONG BEFORE WE'RE ALL USING THESE ON EARTH. SOME OF OUR PEOPLE HAVE REPLICATED THEM FOR FIELDWORK IN THE EASTERN DEAD ZONES. ANOTHER FINE PRODUCT BROUGHT TO YOU BY THE RDA!

Alpha Centauri System

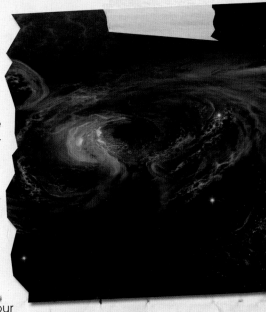

LOCATION: 4.37 light-years from Earth

DESCRIPTION: Alpha Centauri, the brightest "star" in the constellation of Centaurus, when seen through a telescope, is, in fact, three stars orbiting around one another. This triple star system consists of two sun-like stars, Alpha Centauri A, Alpha Centauri B, and a red dwarf, Alpha Centauri C.

Alpha Centauri is a trinary star system, and Earth's closest stellar neighbor outside the solar system. Alpha Centauri A (or ACA to astronomers) is the largest member, at about 20 percent larger than our sun. ACA is only notable because it serves as the sun for Pandora, the home of the only other sentient race discovered to date.

Alpha Centauri B (ACB) is about 15 percent smaller than our sun, and noticeably orange because it is five hundred kelvins cooler than its neighboring star. Alpha Centauri C (ACC) is a red dwarf, only 20 percent of the size of the sun and less than half its temperature. ACC gives off only a dim red glow instead of the bright yellow glare of the sun and ACA.

DISCOVERY

Early telescopic and unmanned exploration showed the ACA was full of suprises. The planet Coeus, which is located in the center of ACA's habitable zone, sported a huge eye-shaped storm, many times larger than Jupiter's Great Red Spot. Astronomers renamed the planet "Polyphemus" after the one-eyed cyclops encountered by Odysseus, the hero of Homer's epic poem.

More striking than Polyphemus's huge storm were its moons: clouds and oceans were visible on several of the moons larger

than 6,437 kilometers in diameter. Remote sensing revealed nitrogen-oxygen atmospheres on the fifth and sixth moons; this type of atmosphere could only be produced by carbon-cycle lifeforms. Though some of the other large satellites had significant bodies of surface water, their thinner atmospheres were mostly nitrogen and carbon dioxide, which is an indication of lifelessness.

Polyphemus

LOCATION: The second of three gas giant planets orbiting the star Alpha Centauri A

DESCRIPTION: Smaller than Saturn. One of its moons, Pandora, is home to the Na'vi.

Polyphemus is a gas giant planet, similar to our own Saturn, but without its rings. But unlike that planet, which is located in the outer reaches of our solar system, Polyphemus orbits Alpha Centauri A at a distance comparable to Earth's orbit of the Sun. Because Polyphemus formed in a higher-temperature environment than Saturn, it is composed of a much larger proportion of helium and other heavier elements, and has a greater mass for its size.

Polyphemus has more prominent banding than Saturn, although its bands are not as spectacular as Jupiter's. But Polyphemus has a vortex storm far exceeding Jupiter's Great Red Spot in size and turbulence. Auroral activity is near-continuous and intense enough to be visible in daylight. When magnetic flux tubes form and link to various satellites, they too display brilliant auroral bands in the moons' polar regions, where the tubes' flux joins the global ones.

Polyphemus has fourteen satellites, including Pandora. The two outer moons orbit in the opposite direction from all the others.

The chemical "stew" in its atmosphere is stirred by convection currents and gale-force winds produced by the planet's rapid rotation. The result is a brilliant display of an ever-changing pattern of colored cloud belts and rotating storms.

A large and a small planetoid share Polyphemus's orbit, occupying the pseudostable Lagrangian Points L4 and L5, located 60 degrees ahead of and behind Polyphemus.

UNOBTANIUM

FUNCTION: Vital for matter-antimatter energy generators, interstellar and deep space travel, Superluminal Communicationss, and operation of maglev trains

PROPERTIES: A high-temperature superconductor that is capable of both repelling magnetic fields and trapping them within itself

APPEARANCE: Metallic, silver-gray cubic crystal

LOCATION: A naturally occurring substance found only on Pandora

Modern civilization is dependent on superconductive technology to help fuel the economy. In addition, many specialized applications such as Superluminal Communications and computer hyperchip manufacturing would be impossible without it.

When the world's first high-temperature superconductor was created in the late twentieth century, it proved to be useless because of inherent instabilities. Further efforts proved futile, and researchers finally termed their goal "unobtainium" (the spelling was later changed to "unobtanium" to conform to chemical element naming, although unobtanium is a compound, not an element). There matters stood until the first unmanned exploration vehicle reached Alpha Centauri A and discovered deposits of a high-temperature superconducting substance on an Earth-like moon named Pandora—unobtanium had been obtained at last.

When the first sample of unobtanium was extracted from its ore, it was found to contain an extremely strong magnetic field. This was a complete violation of everything then known about super-conductors—they repel magnetic fields. Scientists were baffled until microscanning revealed the first of unobtanium's many secrets—unlike the fragile crystals of human-created superconducting compounds, the substance found on Pandora was a stable quasicrystal with its atoms arranged in a never-repeating but orderly pattern with fivefold symmetry. This structure is not only mechanically rugged but also has microscopic voids in the quasicrystalline structure that contain the magnetic flux lines.

Pandoran unobtanium beat the best superconductor that humans had ever created. It remained superconducting up to its melting point of 1,516°C (2,761°F). Unobtanium was also incredibly resistant to magnetic fields, remaining superconducting when surrounded by a field of one billion gauss (one hundred thousand teslas), more than a thousand times better than any Terran material.

Researchers theorize that billions of years ago, when the planets and satellites of the Alpha Centauri system were condensing from the primordial stellar nebula, a Mars-sized planetesimal may have crashed into the still-molten Pandora. The moon's nickel-iron core was disrupted. The high temperatures and pressures produced in the collision far exceeded anything wrought by human technology. These forces interacted with Polyphemus's intense magnetic field and created conditions suitable for the production of this unique substance.

Refined product has current market value of 40 million dollars per kilo. Vital to Earth economy.

THE DESTRUCTION OF PANDORA WILL
CONTINUE AS LONG AS THE RDA CAN
SUCCESSFULLY SUPPRESS ANY ATTEMPT TO
DEVELOP A TERRAN ALTERNATIVE TO
UNOBTANIUM. THIS MATERIAL IS THE
ULTIMATE MOTIVATION FOR EXPLORATION AND
COLONIZATION OF PANDORA AND REPRESSION
OF THE NA'VI. BRUTAL BLACK MARKET HELPS
FUND TERRORIST GROUPS. ONE SWISS MOBSTER
REPORTEDLY WEARS RING MADE
FROM UNOBTANIUM.

SUPERCONDUCTIVITY

Superconductivity is the property of certain materials to con-
duct electricity with absolutely no resistance and thus no
loss of electrical energy dissipated as heat in the wire. It is a
manifestation of quantum physics, rather than just the normal
reduction of electrical resistance with temperature. Superconducting materials also have unique magnetic properties.

Modern civilization is dependent on superconductive
technology for the major areas of power generation, transportation, and interstellar travel. In addition, many specialized applications such as Superluminal Communications
and computer hyperchip manufacturing would be impossible without it.

Ordinary electrical conductivity occurs when the outer (valence) electrons of an atom are not strongly bound
and can be freed with very little effort. Metals are the prime
example of a conductive material, particularly copper, sil-
ver, and gold. However, the resistance of metal wire is not
zero. Some of the electrical energy is converted to heat as
the current passes through the wire. This requires that an
electrical conductor have a large diameter in order to carry
large amounts of current, both to reduce the overall resistance and to prevent the wire from heating to its melting
point.

Superconductivity is the result of an entirely different
phenomenon from that which occurs in ordinary conduc-
tors at lowered temperatures. Even now, in the twenty-
second century, it is not completely understood. In essence,
superconductivity requires that electrons carrying electrical
energy pair up and move in perfect unison, unlike those in a

normal conductor, which jostle one another in a mad rush toward the finish line. Superconductivity was initially discovered only at temperatures very near absolute zero and was considered merely a laboratory curiosity. But over the centuries, substances were created that superconducted at higher and higher temperatures. Today, they function at well above the boiling point of water (100°C = 212°F).

Whenever an electrical current flows, it creates a magnetic field. One of the properties of superconducting material is the ability to repel such fields. The repulsion is so strong that a piece of superconducting material will float on a magnetic field.

Much research has been done to improve superconductors' resistance to magnetic penetration. As of today, unobtanium has by far the best performance. Under certain circumstances, it is even possible to trap an intense magnetic field within unobtanium. This unique and baffling property has opened up many new applications and areas for research.

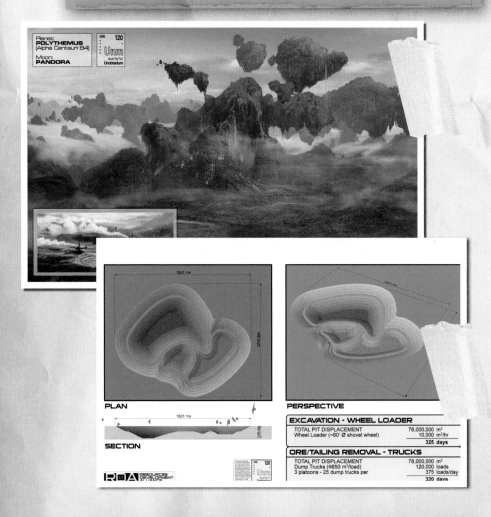

Planet:
POLYTHEMUS
(Alpha Centauri B4)
Moon:
PANDORA

120
Unm
formerly
Unobtanium

PLAN

1501.1m

SECTION

135.0m

1501.1m

1212.5m

PERSPECTIVE

EXCAVATION - WHEEL LOADER

TOTAL PIT DISPLACEMENT	78,000,000 m³
Wheel Loader (~60' Ø shovel wheel)	10,000 m³/hr
	325 days

ORE/TAILING REMOVAL - TRUCKS

TOTAL PIT DISPLACEMENT	78,000,000 m³
Dump Trucks (@650 m³/load)	120,000 loads
3 platoons - 25 dump trucks per	375 loads/day
	320 days

RDA RESOURCES
DEVELOPMENT

120
Unm

STONE ARCHES

SIZE: Various. Largest are 300 meters in height and span 500 meters in width.

COMPOSITION: Composite rock with high concentration of iron ore

DESCRIPTION: One of Pandora's signature landforms. Formed when Pandora cooled from molten state. Loops of intense magnetic fields, which were created by unobtanium, shaped the melted rock. The rock then hardened to create the formations. Surrounding rock has eroded over the millennia to reveal the arches.

RDA miners use arches to help locate unobtanium deposits. Arches also serve to warn pilots of the nexus of intense magnetic fields that can confound their navigation systems and alter operation of aircraft.

THE HALLELUJAH MOUNTAINS

DESCRIPTION: A group of stone monoliths that hover thousands of meters above the surface of Pandora

SIZE: Various, from boulder-sized to more than 16 kilometers across

Floating mountains and stone arches are Pandora's two signature landforms. The Hallelujah Mountains are considered sacred by the Na'vi. They are the staging ground for *Iknimaya*, a treacherous but fundamental rite of passage in which a young Na'vi must select, capture, and successfully bond with one of the *ikran* (banshees) who nest there.

The first human explorers to see images of the floating mountains were awestruck, as are all humans lucky enough to have seen the phenomenon. The sight of billions of tons of rock floating as weightlessly as a cloud was inexplicable, almost hallucinatory.

After the initial unobtanium deposit was found, its superconducting properties provided the first clue to help unravel the mystery of the floating mountains.

Scientists assumed that the phenomenon must have something to do with the intense magnetic fields in the area, but they had no explanation for their source. The answer was found as a result of site surveys conducted by RDA geologists who linked unobtanium to the magnetic fields. When accurate maps of ground magnetic isobars were studied, they revealed a magnetic field gradient that surrounded each floating mountain with a perimeter of increased field strength that acted like a "magnetic fence." This explained their stable positions, but raised the new question of how this situation came about.

Two schools of thought arose. The first, and by far the largest, originally propounded by Dimitri Pechta of Luna's Armstrong University, was that some sort of positive feedback mechanism during Pandora's molten phase attracted large areas of like magnetic fields in an unobtanium deposit, and their mutual repulsion finally pushed a large chunk of unobtanium-containing matter away, to hang in the air until it cooled and solidified. The ordinary nonmagnetic rock was

denser, and settled to the bottom of the molten mass as it cooled, forming the necessary ballast, like the heavy keel of a boat. The crater left behind at the top of the monolith was therefore deficient in the superconductor and its associated magnetic field. This left a ring of a stronger magnetic field around the circumference of the crater, which in turn restrained the floating mountain.

The second, and minority, opinion held that the finely balanced floating mountains required some sort of conscious supervision during their creation. They directed their attention to the worldwide links between the various life-forms and the satellite's ecology, as represented by the spiritual deity and natural phenomenon the Na'vi refer to as "Eywa."

THE PUBLIC KNOWS NOTHING ABOUT THIS: THE RDA IS DESTROYING EVEN THESE PANDORAN MASTERPIECES. A SCORE OF PERSONNEL WERE KILLED DURING UNOBTANIUM EXCAVATION, WHEN A SHIP-SIZED FORMATION ABOVE THEM SUDDENLY INVERTED AND CRASHED DOWN ON THE WORKERS. REMOVAL OF UNOBTANIUM HAD LIKELY DISRUPTED MAGNETIC FIELDS AROUND THE MOUNTAIN. BUT SOME MAINTAIN THAT IT WAS AN ACT OF "BALANCING" INITIATED BY EYWA.

The floating masses will sometimes crash together, thus the Na'vi name "Thundering Rocks." Humans named them the "Hallelujah Mountains," because they portend the wealth of unobtanium.

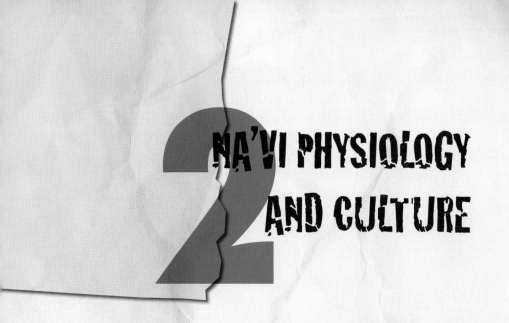

2 NA'VI PHYSIOLOGY AND CULTURE

Thriving on a moon known for its abundant life, the exotic-looking Na'vi are, on average, three meters tall with smooth cyan-colored skin, feline-shaped eyes, and sweeping prehensile tails. They are the only known species outside of Earth discovered to date to have human-like consciousness and intelligence. They have developed a vibrant, complex, and sophisticated culture based on a profound spiritual connection to their moon, to one another, and to the encompassing "spirit" they call Eywa.

The operative concept for the Na'vi is balance. Their lives express this balance in body, mind, and spirit. Pandora meets all the needs of its inhabitants. The Na'vi respect her life-sustaining bounty and are socially organized to maintain it. That social organization is evident in tribal distribution and geographic location—from the plains-based direhorse clans to forest clans living under the canopy. Population of all life-forms is in perfect dynamic equilibrium, with an organic and natural symmetry that makes concepts like overpopulation, poverty, or homelessness unintelligible.

Na'vi

COMMON NAME: Na'vi

NA'VI NAME: *Na'vi,* or "the people"

TAXONOMY: *Homo pandorus*

RANGE: Various biomes of Pandora. Population concentrated in rainforest regions. Outlying clans have been detected on each continent and in subarctic, swampland, and mountainous regions.

ANATOMY: Smooth skin is iridescent, cyan color. Long, prehensile tail. Skull is proportionately small, high cheekbones, feline ears, and a protruding snout. Bioluminescent markings for identification, mood display. Average life span is similar to that of a human. Despite skin color, Na'vi have red blood.

FEEDING ECOLOGY: Omnivore. Hunter and gatherer with incipient agriculture, including brewing.

SIZE: Average male is 3 meters tall, females slightly smaller.

Although their society is essentially Neolithic, the Na'vi have developed a complex culture based on a profound spiritual connection among all creatures, and to the deity they call Eywa. They are superb artisans who celebrate the interconnectedness of nature through storytelling, song, dance, and crafts.

They are expert hunters and gatherers. In many respects, the Na'vi body is almost humanlike (and, even by human standards, beautiful). The waist is narrow and elongated. The shoulders are very wide, creating a V-shaped upper back. The neck is twice as long as an average human. The body overall is more slender than the average human. But the musculature is sharply defined, giving no sense of emaciation despite the thin proportions. (They have roughly four times the strength of the average human.) Their almond-shaped eyes are large and hypersensitive to various bands of light. For balancing their long torso and legs, the Na'vi have a long, prehensile tail. They can traverse the landscape on the surface as well as from tree branch to tree branch.

The abundant flora and fauna of Pandora have ensured a steady population of Na'vi; it is hypothesized that there was little Darwinian pressure to adapt new traits, which in turn has led to a slower evolutionary process than on Earth. Indeed, studies indicate that the number of Na'vi have remained remarkably consistent over the eons. The widespread access to natural resources has also helped limit (but not eliminate) warfare among the various Na'vi clans.

Generally peaceful, but ferocious in defense of home, clan, and family.

QUEUE

At first glance, a human might think of the Na'vi queue as simply a long, rather ostentatious hair braid. This seemingly conventional braid actually sheathes a remarkably intricate system of neural ten-

drils that can be connected to similar structures of other life-forms. This connection allows a Na'vi to sense the energetic and kinetic signals broadcast by creatures, plants, and even the moon itself. It is believed that the queue also allows the Na'vi to access the neural network that envelops the entire moon, and thus the collective wisdom of all Pandoran life.

It is difficult to overstate the importance of the queue to the spiritual and physical well-being of the Na'vi. It is used on a daily basis to connect to animals that are vital to the success and protection of the clan; the direhorse and the mountain banshee both come under the sway of the Na'vi through use of the queue.

A HUMANOID SINGULARLY ATTUNED TO ITS ENVIRONMENT, THE NA'VI DO NOT SEE THEMSELVES AS SEPARATE FROM NATURE, BUT RATHER AN INTEGRAL PART OF IT. HUMANS HAD A SIMILAR INTERCONNECTEDNESS WITH NATURE LONG AGO.

Na'vi Mating Practices

The Na'vi are monogamous creatures who mate for life. The mechanics of reproduction are similar to that of humans and other Terran mammals. But their unique physiology provides the Na'vi with a level of intimacy unknown on Earth. Cultural anthorpologists believe that when an appropriate mate has been selected (which can take many years), the male and female Na'vi will connect queues to create an emotional bond that lasts a lifetime. The intertwining of queues is both highly erotic and profoundly spiritual, but does not in itself lead to reproduction.

BABY CARRIER

FUNCTION: Carrying infants close to body

NAVI NAME: *Iveh k'nivi s'dir*

SIZE: Various lengths, usually no shorter than 4 meters of stripping to allow for complete wrapping

MATERIALS AND CONSTRUCTION: Soft sturmbeest leather with fur, cut in strips, tanned and softened

A tight frontal wrap keeps Na'vi infants close to their mother's or father's body. The carrier keeps babies warm and allows the parent to run, climb, and carry out domestic activities. The wrap also helps socialize Na'vi children, who are face-to-face with their parents from their first days and thus learn appropriate facial cues and gestures. Most Na'vi couples have one to three children, although there are exceptions.

EVEN AS OUR OWN POPULATION SPIRALS OUT OF CONTROL, THE NATURAL BALANCE OF PANDORA ENSURES A CONSTANT EQUILIBRIUM BETWEEN BIRTH AND DEATH.

Octal Arithmetic

DESCRIPTION: The Na'vi system of counting, based on the number eight, developed because the Na'vi have only four digits on each hand.

FUNCTION: Used in daily life for supply of foodstuffs, matériel, hunting

Humans use a base-10 (decimal) number system, composed of ten digits: 0, 1, 2, 3, 4, 5, 6, 7, 8, and 9. A second column added to the left uses these same digits to indicate values ten times greater. Digits in a third column have a value a hundred (10 x 10) times greater, and so on.

The Na'vi have a version of "This Little Piggy," the game in which Earth children have their toes grabbed one by one as a poem is recited. The Na'vi version has only four lines and refers to a viperwolf cub, not a pig.

E.g., **2,475** = (2 x 1000) + (4 x 100) + (7 x 10) + (5 x 1) = 2,000 + 400 + 70 + 5 = 2,475.

Na'vi use a base-8 (octal) number system, composed of eight digits: **0, 1, 2, 3, 4, 5, 6,** and **7.** A second column added to the left uses these same digits to indicate values eight times greater. Digits in a third column have a value sixty-four (8 x 8) times greater, and so on.

E.g., **2,475** = (**2** x 512) + (**4** x 64) + (**7** x 8) + (**5** x 1) = 1,024 + 256 + 56 + 5 = 1,341.

Early in the history of their language, the Na'vi had no words for numbers higher than *vofu* (16), the sum of all the fingers and toes on their body. Anything more was simply called *pxay* (many)."

Note that octal numbers are often confused with decimal numbers. Unless a numeral "8" or "9" is present, there is no way to tell them apart.

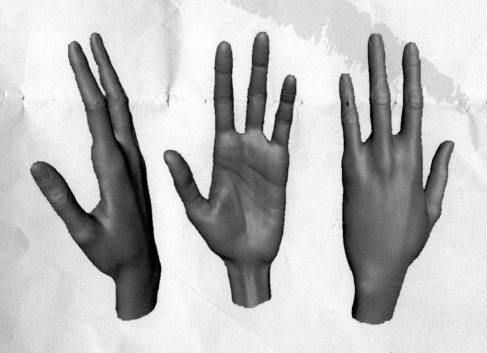

Old School House: RDA educational center for Na'vi sited in jungle clearing 2.25 kilometers northeast of Hell's Gate. Focus on English language for Na'vi children. Accessible by armored vehicles, Samsons, or avatars on foot.

HOMETREE

FUNCTION: Spiritual and physical home of the Omaticaya clan

NA'VI NAME: *Kelutral*

SIZE: More than 325 meters in height, roughly 57 meters in diameter, with a base of 122 meters

There are hundreds of disparate Na'vi clans on Pandora. Some of the clans, including the Omaticaya, live in ancient trees that are two to three times the height of the Terran redwoods that once covered the Pacific Northwest. The circumference of Hometree is great enough to house dozens of clan members. The tree is honeycombed with natural hollows and alcoves in which the Na'vi sleep, eat, weave, dance, and celebrate their connection to Eywa. Like many sacred sites on Pandora, Hometree sits above a large deposit of unobtanium.

As a rite of passage, young Omaticayan hunters earn the right to carve a bow from a branch of Hometree after Uniltaron.

BLADDER LANTERN

FUNCTION: A light source in Na'vi villages, or wherever light is needed

NA'VI NAME: *Tmi nat'sey*, or "food here"

SIZE AND WEIGHT: Roughly 1 meter high, .5 kilograms

MATERIALS AND CONSTRUCTION: Lantern consists of the stomach, or thin-skinned internal organs of various animals, dried and sewn with twine and leather. The organ's interior is coated with nectar to attract an indigenous glowing insect similar to a Terran firefly. Those insects, in turn, attract more of their kind, perpetuating and increasing the lantern's glow.

Though the Na'vi have naturally excellent night vision, they enjoy the calming glow provided by these lanterns inside Hometree.

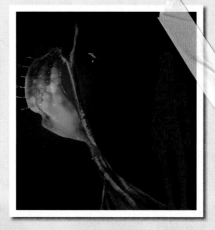

HOMETREE SONGS

FUNCTION: To accompany hearth and home activities

NA'VI NAME: *Kelutral tìrol,* or "Hometree songs"

PERFORMANCE STYLE: Various

The Na'vi people have no indigenous musical theory; they do not analyze or codify their musical creations. Songs come to the Na'vi through dreams, while wandering alone, or while linked with the consciousness of Pandora through their queues. Na'vi do not claim ownership; the songs belong to all.

Unlike aboriginal cultures on Earth, both men and women join in songs that revolve around home and hearth activities, such as weaving, cooking, child-rearing, and playing games with children. The songs are led by fathers and adult women who had children. They use a very wide vocal range, often encompassing three octaves (although they do not use that concept). Many Hometree songs involve overlapping, cascading musical lines, with each performer singing the same basic melody but joining the song at different points, with different tempi and rhythms, a style sometimes referred to as heterophony (commonly found on Earth in Eastern musical tradition).

It must be noted that the theoretical information given here is the result of observation and analysis by xenomusicologists. There has been no confirmation of musical theories by the Na'vi themselves. They do not recognize any theoretical basis other than Eywa and are reluctant to discuss their music with outsiders. An Earth-style musicological analysis would make absolutely no sense to them, and they believe the study of music to be a frivolous activity.

THE BLUE FLUTE

FUNCTION: Guardian spirit played only on most sacred occasions

NA'VI NAME: *Omati s'ampta*

SIZE AND WEIGHT: Roughly 3 meters long, 18 kilograms

MATERIALS AND CONSTRUCTION: Hollowed branch from Hometree, one finger hole drilled near top

It is interesting to note that, although the Omaticaya calls itself "the Clan of the Blue Flute," the instrument referenced is, at least as described to researchers, not actually a flute. (Some researchers attribute this to a lack of nuance on the part of the Terran translator.) Nor is it used as a musical instrument. There is only one in existence, kept carefully within the limbs of Hometree. It serves as a guardian spirit and a concrete representation of the connection of the Na'vi with the Hometree. The flute (actually a one-holed trumpet in terms of playing techniques) is of ancient ancestry. Na'vi mythology purports that Eywa plucked a branch from the Hometree, created the Blue Flute, and gave it to the Omaticaya with the intent that it be used as a device to communicate with her or the spirits of ancestors who have passed on. Xenomusicologists believe that it is heard only on the most sacred of occasions, including the alignment of nearby planets and is played only by the *olo'eyktan* (male clan leader).

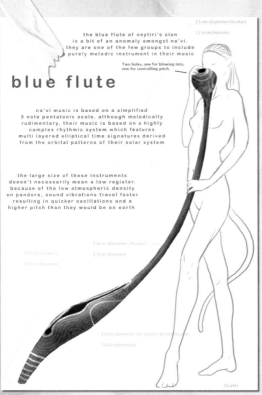

the blue flute of neytiri's clan is a bit of an anomaly amongst na'vi. they are one of the few groups to include a purely melodic instrument in their music

Two holes, one for blowing into, one for controlling pitch.

blue flute

na'vi music is based on a simplified 5 note pentatonic scale. although melodically rudimentary, their music is based on a highly complex rhythmic system which features multi layered elliptical time signatures derived from the orbital patterns of their solar system

the large size of these instruments doesn't necessarily mean a low register. because of the low atmospheric density on pandora, sound vibrations travel faster resulting in quicker oscillations and a higher pitch than they would be on earth

21cm diameter(Avatar)
12.6cm(human)

5.6cm diameter (Avatar)
3.5cm (human)

24cm diameter (at widest point)(Avatar)
14.4cm(human)

(Scale)

Flute has never been seen by human researchers or avatars.

HAMMOCKS

FUNCTION: Sleeping, clan bonding

NA'VI NAME: *Eywa k'sey nivi'bri'sta,* or "Eywa cradles everyone"

SIZE: Various, depending on whether it is used by individual, mates, or family

MATERIALS AND CONSTRUCTION: Rope, twine, strong woven mats usually made from beanstalk palm. A large central mat is woven in a decorative pattern, which is then affixed to a rope support structure. The finished hammock is then fastened to branches of Hometree.

The Na'vi prefer to sleep in large groups for physical closeness and comfort. This arrangement also acts as an effective early warning system in the event of danger. Families sleep together on larger hammocks, which are decorated and meticulously constructed for flexibility and strength. The Na'vi call the large family hammock *Eywa k'sey nivi'bri'sta,* which translates roughly into "safe in the arms of Eywa," or, more literally, as "Eywa cradles everyone." For everyday use, the family hammock is known simply as *nivi,* or "us."

Clan members will occasionally sleep singly or with their mates in smaller hammocks. This is socially acceptable as long as the member returns to group sleep, or *k'sey nivi,* within a short period. As attuned as they are to one another, the Na'vi use sleeping arrangements as an accurate barometer of a clan member's emotional health; if a Na'vi is seen to sleep outside the group *(sumin'sey hulleh)* for an extended period, it is generally considered a sign that the clan member is in some kind of distress.

Because of the fine craftsmanship, hammocks can last for more than twenty Terran years. Family elders decide when a new hammock is needed. Construction takes place over a period of months and generates a good deal of enthusiasm within both the family and the clan as a whole; everyone contributes to the effort. A great deal of time is spent in gathering the correct materials, and it is during this process that most of the familial bonding takes place. The construction itself is a relatively informal and straightforward process.

As the hammock nears completion, several ceremonies take place to honor and acknowledge the hard work. When the new hammock is finally installed and the old one is removed, there is a ceremony in which the old hammock is burned on a pyre in a serious, respectful manner. At the end of this ceremony, the family puts on a celebration with food and dance in honor of the moment of renewal.

THE NA'VI HAVE A CLOSENESS AND COMMUNITY THAT WE, IN OUR SOLITARY, HIGH-TECH SQUALOR, HAVE LOST ON EARTH. IF WE LEARN NOTHING ELSE, WE MUST LEARN AGAIN TO TRUST WHEN EVERYTHING IN OUR DIMINISHED LIVES SAYS WE CAN'T.

Loom

FUNCTION: Weaving items such as cloth, hammocks, mats, hanging decorations

NA'VI NAME: *Ulivi mari'tsey mak'dini'to*

SIZE AND WEIGHT: Various sizes depending on scale and type of project

MATERIALS AND CONSTRUCTION: Framework of rope and wood suspended from branches of Hometree and secured to ground by simple wooden crank system

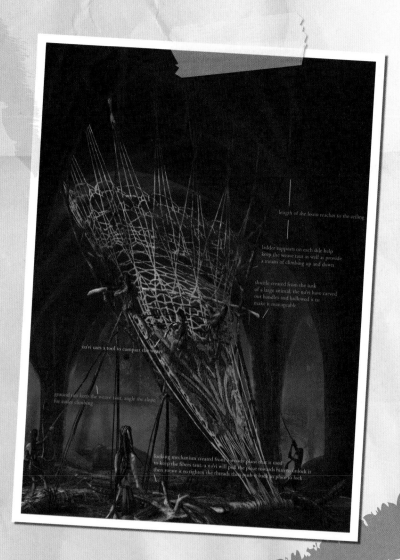

length of the loom reaches to the ceiling

ladder supports on each side help keep the weave taut as well as provide a means of climbing up and down

shuttle created from the tusk of a large animal; the na'vi have carved out handles and hollowed it to make it manageable

na'vi uses a tool to compact the weave

ground rods keep the weave taut; angle the slope for easier climbing

locking mechanism created from a woody plant that is used to keep the fibers taut; a na'vi will pull the piece towards him to unlock it then rotate it to tighten the threads then push it back in place to lock

While other Na'vi clans on Pandora organize themselves around carving or pottery, the Omaticaya are renowned for their brilliant textiles. Thus the loom plays a key role in the daily life of the clan. The largest of the Omaticayan looms is more massive than a Terran pipe organ. This *mas'kit nivi sa'nok*, or "mother loom" is given a place of honor in the common area of Hometree.

The Na'vi word for loom, *ulivi mari'tsey mak'dini'to*, translates roughly into "branches of the tree look to each other for strength," or "many branches together are strong." Depending on the type of textile produced, the loom can also be referred to as *Eywa s'ilivi mas'kit nivi* (or just *mas'kit nivi*) which translates into "Eywa's wisdom is revealed to all of us." This evocation of Eywa is a clear indication of the loom's importance in Na'vi culture. It is also a compelling description of Eywa, who, in this context, is depicted as a kind of cosmic weaver who brings the disparate elements of Pandora together into a harmonious whole.

Weavers will often sing of these themes while at the loom.

WEAVING SONG

The rhythm of rain and sun,	*Tompayä kato, tsawkeyä kato,*
Of night and day,	*Trrä sì txonä,*
The rhythm of the years,	*S(ì) ayzìsìtä kato,*
And the beat of the hearts,	*Sì'ekong te'lanä,*
Hearts of the people	*Te'lanä le-Na'vi*
Fills me,	*Oeru teya si,*
Fills me.	*Oeru teya si.*
I weave the rhythm	*Katot täftxu oel*
In yellow and blue,	*Nìean nìrim,*
The rhythm of the years,	*Ayzìsìtä kato,*
The spiral of the lives,	*'Ìheyu sìreyä,*
The spiral of the lives,	*'Ìheyu sìreyä,*
Lives of the people,	*Sìreyä le-Na'vi,*
Fills me,	*Oeru teya si,*
Fills me.	*Oeru teya si.*

I'VE HEARD THEIR MUSIC. I HEAR IT IN MY DREAMS—SWEET AND SOFT AND INFUSED WITH A SILENCE ALIEN TO THE POUNDING DISSONANCE THAT COUNTS OUT OUR DAYS ON EARTH.

FIRE PIT

FUNCTION: Food preparation

NA'VI NAME: *Mreki u'lito*

SIZE: Anywhere from 3 to 5 meters in length

MATERIALS AND CONSTRUCTION: Rocks arranged around a sunken earthen pit. Firewood is first charcoalized for use in the pit. Fire pits are usually an elongated shape so that larger cross stones can be placed across the coals perpendicularly.

Much like the ancient campfires and hearths of old Earth, Na'vi fire pits are centers of clan social life. Na'vi children grow up near the warmth of the fire and hear stories of their ancestors. Not all the discussion is serious. The cooks gossip about potential matings and joke about which hunter brought in the smallest hexapede. According to clan lore, the fire has been kept going, at least at ember level, for several generations. Even if this is not the literal truth, it is considered a lapse to have a fire that is not ready to quickly accommodate a successful hunt; the Na'vi believe that it is vital to honor the animal that gave up its life for the good of the clan. A fire turned to ash might indicate a lack of respect for both animal and hunter.

NA'VI FIRE-PIT

Stone slabs over stone-bed fire-pit.

PLAN VIEW-

SIDE VIEW-

Flat stones form bowl for embers.

Entire clan's food is prepared and cooked in waves on fire-pit, kept perpetually lit and fanned.

Packed, wet earth insulates Hometree from pit's heat.

LEAF PLATE

FUNCTION: Food tray used to transport drinking bowls during formal ceremonies, festivities

NA'VI NAME: *Sumin jiit'luy,* or *ulu'tah inib'sey mulsi*

SIZE AND WEIGHT: Roughly 1 meter in length, or Na'vi shoulder-width

MATERIALS AND CONSTRUCTION: Animal shell and bone, leaves, wood, reeds, twigs, and twine are formed into a wide, shallow basket

Na'vi etiquette and tradition dictates that these trays are passed to every participant of a social gathering or ritual. One should not take a bowl, which is used for a mildly intoxicating drink, off the tray for his or her own use. Instead, one must hold the tray and allow another adjacent clan member to take the bowl and place it before the drinker. Only then can one drink from the cup. During festive occasions, children enjoy following the tray around the circle so that they can be the one to place the bowl in front of the tray holder.

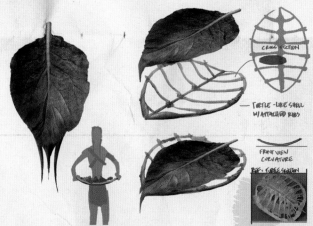

CROSS SECTION

— TURTLE-LIKE SHELL W/ ATTACHED RIBS

FRONT VIEW CURVATURE

REF. TURTLE SKELETON

THE NA'VI ARE A DIGNIFIED AND CULTURED RACE, WITH A HIGHLY SOPHISTICATED ETIQUETTE. BENT ON THE TACTICAL AND STRATEGIC "DEHUMANIZATION" OF THESE NOBLE BEINGS, THE RDA PRESENTS THEM AS SAVAGES AND SEEKS IMPUNITY FOR THEIR SYSTEMATIC RELOCATION. THE NA'VI ARE MORE "HUMAN"—AND CERTAINLY POSSESS MORE "HUMANITY"—THAN MOST RDA EXECUTIVES.

PERSONAL BELONGINGS RACK

FUNCTION: Rack for personal items, including clothing, jewelry, and tools, etc.

NA'VI NAME: *P'ah s'ivil chey,* or, informally, *chey*

SIZE AND WEIGHT: Roughly 1 meter wide by .75 meter in height. Weight depends on size and number of stone weights used for stabilization.

MATERIALS AND CONSTRUCTION: Carved hardwood, attached with leather straps, often decorated with shells, colored stones

By tradition, a Na'vi cannot build his or her own rack. Instead, they must be given one as a gift from a friend or family member. The long hours and craftsmanship needed to create the racks are considered powerful symbols of filial and familial love. It is believed that the ritual helps strengthen clan bonding.

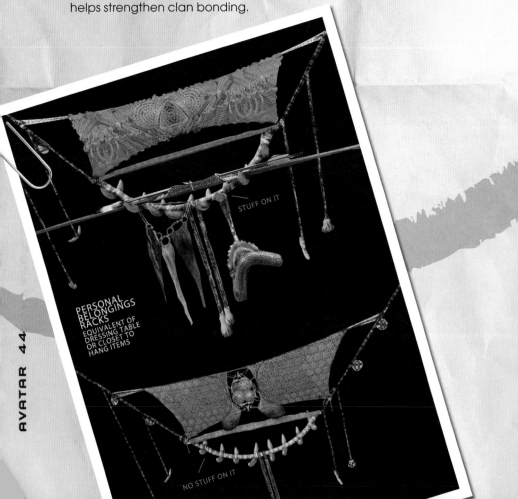

STUFF ON IT

PERSONAL
BELONGINGS
RACKS
EQUIVALENT OF
DRESSING TABLE
OR CLOSET TO
HANG ITEMS

NO STUFF ON IT

CEREMONIAL BOW

FUNCTION: Ceremonial, but can be used for hunting

SIZE AND WEIGHT: 2.9 meters long, 3.7 kilograms

MATERIALS AND CONSTRUCTION: Shaped wood from Hometree, string is made of animal gut

DESCRIPTION: This ranged bow is primarily designed for ceremony by clan elders, but it is crafted to the peak of Na'vi design and thus functions perfectly in hunt or battle. This bow is fashioned in honor of the direhorse, these exquisite bows are usually handed down from generation to generation and become powerful symbols of survival, continuity, and tradition.

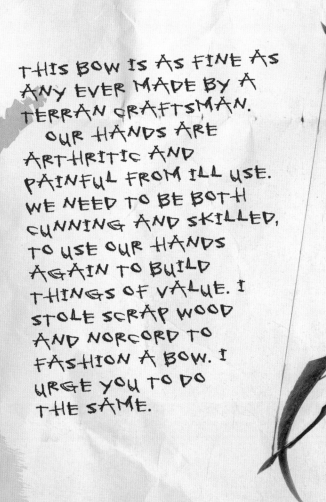

THIS BOW IS AS FINE AS ANY EVER MADE BY A TERRAN CRAFTSMAN. OUR HANDS ARE ARTHRITIC AND PAINFUL FROM ILL USE. WE NEED TO BE BOTH CUNNING AND SKILLED, TO USE OUR HANDS AGAIN TO BUILD THINGS OF VALUE. I STOLE SCRAP WOOD AND NORCORD TO FASHION A BOW. I URGE YOU TO DO THE SAME.

War Drum

FUNCTION: Accompaniment to pre-battle ritual dance, warning signals

SIZE AND WEIGHT: 3 meter in height, 4 meters in diameter, roughly 75 kilograms

MATERIALS AND CONSTRUCTION: Structure of branches, covered on both sides with tanned hexapede hides. Filled with water. Beating stick is made from smoothed branch the size of a Terran baseball bat.

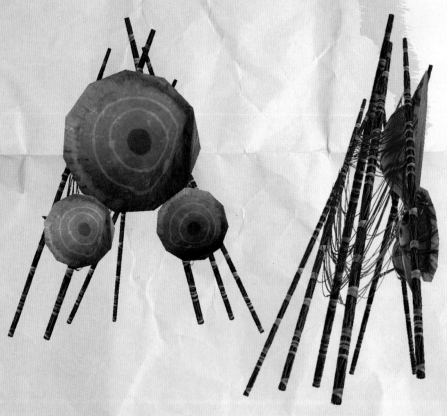

The different warning rhythms played on it are associated with specific dangers to the Na'vi and are used to signal for help. Because of its association with danger, the drum is also used to accompany ritual

prebattle dances. The drum is kept accessible at all times in an alcove off the communal area of Hometree. A small branch of Hometree is dropped into the drum as a symbol of the precious resources for which the Na'vi fight.

Amplified by the water inside, this large drum's volume is sufficient to warn all Na'vi within a six-mile radius of approaching danger. When the drum is struck with its large smooth wooden beater, the water inside sloshes against the taut hexapede hides, amplifying the volume and changing the resonant pitch of the sound.

Some of the warning rhythms played on the drum represent different dangers; other rhythms indicate the direction from which the danger approaches. One rhythm is played when a Na'vi is in mortal danger and in need of help. Historically, during pre-battle rituals, if the enemy was known, the Na'vis used associated warning rhythms during ritual dances. Na'vi children learn the different signals from an early age.

The more recent incursions by humans necessitated the addition of another warning rhythm. It is theorized that the warning rhythm for Terrans is based on the Na'vi word *skx'awng,* a highly derogatory term that is more or less analogous to "moron," or "one who does not *see.*"

WE'VE BROKEN THE GENETIC CODE BUT WE STILL CAN'T FIGURE OUT THE SUBTLE MESSAGE OF A SIMPLE NA'VI DRUMBEAT. MAY HAVE APPLICATION FOR MESSAGE ENCRYPTION.

3 FAUNA OF PANDORA

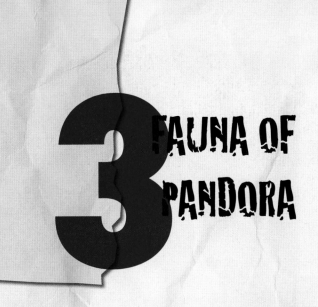

The beauty and brutality of Pandoran fauna continues to delight humans and baffle xenobotanists. Consider the slinger, a bizarre creature that can, quite literally, lose its head in the search for food. Or the medusa, a massive jellyfish-like creature that floats on the Pandoran winds like an errant birthday balloon. Or the thanator, an apex predator that could have easily dispensed with a *T. rex* at the height of the Cretaceous Period.

The bones of all Pandoran animals are comprised of a biologically produced carbon fiber composite. Many animals have adapted to the dense Pandoran atmosphere with a high-performance breathing system that, like a xenobiologic hot rod, takes in air through one opening and exhales through another.

The array of life—from single cell to sentient Na'vi—is as comprehensive as that of pre-industrial Earth. One researcher has remarked that some Pandoran animals that are similar to extinct Earth creatures act as a kind of "window into our biological past." Indeed, we are as stunned by what is familiar (pack dynamics, the presence of herbivore and carnivore, the structure of the food chain), as by what is alien (the neural interface between Na'vi and animal, composite-like cells, the ubiquity of bioluminescence.) With all of our own predators gone or going, we delight in the splendor of claws, chitinous armor, obsidian teeth, and even deadly neurotoxins.

For those lucky few scientists who have reached Pandora, the opportunity to witness these creatures firsthand is the crowning achievement of their careers.

And for the rest of us, the knowledge that such creatures still exist fills us with hope.

ARACHNOID

COMMON NAME: Arachnoid

NA'VI NAME: *Kali'weya*

TAXONOMY: *Scorpiosista virosae*, or "poisonous scorpion"

HABITAT: Rainforest vegetation. Range includes thin band of latitude in rainforest regions of Australis. Other species of arachnoids have been found in almost every region of Pandora, but are apparently absent from areas of intense vulcanism.

ANATOMY: Extended thorax, six two-jointed legs (three on either side of thorax). Similar to Terran scorpion and other arachnids. Tail ends in twin stinger that delivers neurotoxin to prey.

FEEDING ECOLOGY: Usual food source is small insects, but will prey upon small rodents and birds if opportunity arises

SIZE: Up to 18 centimeters long

There are hundreds of arachnid-like species found on Pandora (based on research to date). Only a few of the known species produce a psychoactive venom. Of these, only one, the *Kali'weya*, is used in the *Uniltaron*, or "Dream Hunt," ceremony.

As part of the ritual, a prospective warrior must capture his or her own arachnoid, which is kept in an stone jar built specifically for the task. During the ceremony, the creature is made to sting the warrior in order to induce dreamlike hallucinations that are believed by the Na'vi to foretell the warrior's destiny and reveal his or her spirit animal.

The male arachnoid features dark purple and black markings. Those with dark purple and red markings are female. Arachnoids are slightly bioluminescent, with two lateral lines of bioluminescence on their abdomen.

Despite their fearsome appearance, the arachnoid is a shy creature that would rather flee than fight. Arachnoids have been known to take up residence in Na'vi baskets or, on a rare occasion, in the intricate weaving of a hammock.

To strike effectively, the arachnoid must raise its thorax, which causes the venom sac to empty into the stinger canals. During the Dream Hunt ritual, Na'vi elders evoke a sting by placing the arachnoid against the skin of the prospective warrior.

If left untreated, the sting from an arachnoid is usually fatal for a Na'vi child or elder. It has also caused the death of Na'vi warriors during Uniltaron, although this is a rare occurrence. The pain it creates is excruciating, in any case.

The Na'vi have developed an effective antivenom using the roots of the octoshroom, a detoxifying Pandoran plant that appears to negate the effects of the venom's alkaloids. (Tests are ongoing for potential Earth uses for the antivenom). Many Pandoran creatures have developed an immunity to the venom, and can eat the animal with no ill effects. This helps explain the timid nature of the fierce arachnoid.

USE OF THE VENOM IN RITUALS IS SIMILAR TO CEREMONIES OF ABORIGINAL CULTURES OF NORTH AND SOUTH AMERICA—SEARCH FOR SPIRIT ANIMAL, DESTINY IS UNIVERSAL. MUST ENSURE THAT NA'VI DO NOT SHARE THE FATE OF THE ANCIENT LAKOTA OR THE HOPI.

RDA SCIENTISTS ARE INVOLVED IN CLINICAL TRIALS ON THE MIND-ALTERING EFFECTS OF ARACHNOID VENOM AND PANDORAN GLOW WORMS, FOCUSING ON SUSCEPTIBILITY TO HYPNOSIS AND ITS POSSIBLE MILITARY USE IN CHAIN-OF-COMMAND ISSUES, I.E., HEIGHTENED OBEDIENCE AMONG ITS MERCENARY AND SECURITY FORCES. BE WARY OF RDA ATTEMPTS TO NUMB YOU TO THE REALITIES OF LIFE ON EARTH

STONE JAR

FUNCTION: Container used in ceremonies, most notably during Uniltaron, or "Dream Hunt"

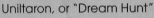

NA'VI NAME: *Chan'tu gor'ek nuuto*

SIZE AND WEIGHT: 25 centimeters tall, roughly 2 kilograms

MATERIALS AND CONSTRUCTION: Local stone is carved, then attached to carved stone base using woven materials, twine, and reeds

This jar holds a small, toxic arachnoid.

Gourd Drums

FUNCTION: Social music, ritual use, including use during Uniltaron

WEIGHT AND SIZE: Various, weighs up to 90 kilograms

MATERIALS AND CONSTRUCTION: Wood, paint, woven materials, leather, rope, gourd, water. Hemispherical floating drum, made from a gourd that has been halved, is inverted into a larger water-filled gourd.

Bioluminescent matter glows through drum skin.

Similar to the *jícara de agua* from Mexico, the Na'vi gourd drum is created by filling a gourd bowl with water and placing an inverted half gourd in the water. The inverted gourd is struck with one wooden drumstick.

A unique element of this drum is an additional smaller drum inserted into a hole cut in the side of the large gourd bowl. This drum is covered with a sturmbeest bladder, a material known for its strength and elasticity. While tapping on the inverted gourd, the player pushes on the bladder, which causes the water level in the gourd bowl to rise, causing the pitch of the drum to change subtly.

When used for the Uniltaron ceremony, a constant rapid tapping of the drum (a sound reminiscent of the ancient peyote songs of Native Americans in the Southwest), while simultaneously pushing the bladder in and out creates a dronelike sound with microtonal fluctuations in pitch. This is related to the microtonal drone heard in the men's part of Na'vi banquet songs thought to represent the spirit of Eywa.

Glow Worms

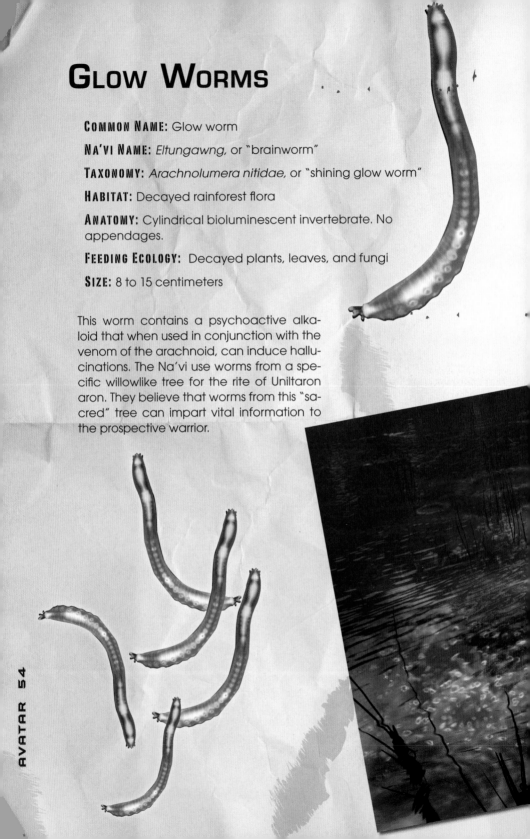

COMMON NAME: Glow worm

NA'VI NAME: *Eltungawng,* or "brainworm"

TAXONOMY: *Arachnolumera nitidae,* or "shining glow worm"

HABITAT: Decayed rainforest flora

ANATOMY: Cylindrical bioluminescent invertebrate. No appendages.

FEEDING ECOLOGY: Decayed plants, leaves, and fungi

SIZE: 8 to 15 centimeters

This worm contains a psychoactive alkaloid that when used in conjunction with the venom of the arachnoid, can induce hallucinations. The Na'vi use worms from a specific willowlike tree for the rite of Uniltaron aron. They believe that worms from this "sacred" tree can impart vital information to the prospective warrior.

ANEMONOID

COMMON NAME: Anemonoid

TAXONOMY: *Cataracta anemonica,* or "waterfall anemonoid"

HABITAT: Ponds and lakes

ANATOMY: Invertebrate-like creature with small toxic tentacles for feeding. Bioluminescence in myriad pastel colors.

FEEDING ECOLOGY: Small fish are attracted by bioluminescence into tentacles and eaten

SIZE: Up to 2 meters in diameter

BIOLUMINESCENCE

DESCRIPTION: Visible light given off by various life-forms, either from chemical reactions within their own bodies, or from symbiotic organisms living within them

FUNCTION: Common among Pandoran plants and animals to allow them to function during the few truly dark nights

Complete darkness is rare on Pandora. The large moon orbits a gas giant planet that in turn orbits a star with a stellar companion. Because of this unusual arrangement, most of Pandora's nights have some illumination; fully dark nights are few and far between. Thus, there was little evolutionary pressure on Pandoran fauna to develop night vision, echolocation, infrared sensors, or other methods of "seeing" in low-light conditions.

Some scientists theorize that nature found another way for Pandoran life-forms to locate and identify one another. Bioluminescence, the production of "cold light" by living organisms, is employed by almost all Pandoran animals and plants to display their shape and location in the absence of external illumination. Even the Na'vi have patterns of glowing dots which, like fingerprints, are unique to each individual. Anemonoid line the dense forest floors and waterways, providing the most light in the night landscape.

Most Pandoran plants and animals glow in a single color, often green or blue, but the entire visible spectrum is represented. The leaves of the warbonnet fern (*Bellicum pennatum*) sport a broad red band near their stems and a blue band toward their tips. There is also a bioluminescent moss that reacts to a footstep by sending out rings of blue-green light, much like ripples on a pond.

The first human explorers were in awe of the spectacle. Later arrivals from the RDA saw it only as another resource to be exploited in the form of exotic Pandoran jewelry and a line of clothing that mimics the phenomenon.

Pervasive and powerful enough to be visible from orbiting spacecraft. Distinct bioluminescent markings on Na'vi allow for identification of fellow clan member in the dark from distances of up to twenty meters.

SYNTHETIC "BIOLUMINESCENT" MARKINGS HAVE PENETRATED THE REMAINS OF OUR CULTURE AND HAVE PROMPTED CERTAIN FORMS OF CULT IDENTITY. BEWARE. RDA AGENTS WITH BIOLUMINESCENT TATTOOS HAVE INFILTRATED GROUPS OF YOUNG TERRANS. THESE ARE AGENTS LOOKING FOR EVIDENCE OF THE MOVEMENT AND DATABASING PRESUMED INVOLVEMENT.

TETRAPTERON

COMMON NAME: Tetrapteron

HABITAT: Wetlands, lakes, rivers, and canopy. Larger in numbers in land-locked water bodies but also found near oceans and rainforest.

ANATOMY: Two pairs of wings, twin tail. Large beak and gullet with glassy teeth.

FEEDING ECOLOGY: Aerial predator, fish-eating

SIZE: Wingspan of nearly 1.5 meters

NOTES: Tracked in continuous flight for nearly thirty-eight hours

The tetraperton is a class of flamingo-like bird that looks almost Earth-like until one notices its four wings, with two on either side. The birds also feature a unique twin tail used for balancing their body weight as they hunt or land.

There are two types of tetrapteron—aquatic and arboreal. Although similar in appearance, the aquatic birds have longer necks and legs for life in wetlands.

The tetrapteron have excellent long-distance vision, and can detect movements as little as 1.25 centimeters from a height of 45 meters. They usually hunt in flocks.

Of all the creatures on Pandora, these seem the most cooperative, both on the hunt and when socializing. While many predators on Pandora nurture their young, none take more care of their offspring with as much attention and duration as the tetrapteron.

Mountain Banshee

COMMON NAME: Mountain banshee

NA'VI NAME: *Ikran*

HABITAT: Mountainous regions of Pandora, including the Hallelujah Mountains

ANATOMY: Leathery membranous wings stretched taut over bone structure. Large distensible jaw. Complex coloring scheme. Teeth are obsidian-like and extremely sharp. Four wings (two aft). Bones comprised of biologically produced carbon fiber composite.

FEEDING ECOLOGY: Aerial predator, carnivore, pack hunter

SIZE: Average wingspan of 13.9 meters

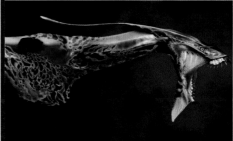
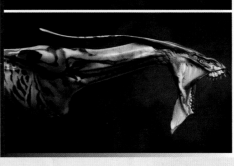

Bonding with a banshee is a dangerous and required rite of passage for all would-be Na'vi warriors. Like the direhorse, a Na'vi can connect to a banshee through a neural interface that allows animal and rider to move with apparent effortlessness through the skies. Unlike the direhorse, however, the banshee will only bond with one Na'vi in its lifetime.

The mountain banshee rookery is high in the Hallelujah Mountains. The largest rookery, which features the biggest specimens (and therefore the best to tame for riding), is in the grottos and outcrops on a sheer cliff face of Mons Veritas, one of the largest of the floating mountains. It is here that the Omaticaya come to select (and be selected by) a banshee for domestication. The bonded mountain banshees nest in branches of Hometree, where they can be close at hand for their Na'vi rider.

The mountain banshee (like its smaller cousin, the forest banshee) is highly adapted for flight. Specially developed muscles attached to the breastbone allow for the powerful strokes needed to achieve lift.

Xenobiologists continue to study the aerodynamics of the banshee. It is believed that all of Pandora's flying animals take advantage of gravity that is lower than Earth's and the increased air density (which requires more force to displace with the downward/rearward stroke of their wings, and thus gives the animal's body more impetus with each flap). The downside is that the denser air is harder to move through, and requires highly efficient streamlining to achieve high flightspeeds.

Like many of Pandora's creatures, the banshee also has a remarkably strong cell structure. This structure, which is an organic carbon fiber, makes its bones much lighter and stronger than any organic Terran equivalent. This in turn allows them to generate more power and lift with every flap.

All flying animals on Pandora, including banshees, are thought to have evolved from sea creatures because of their fishlike jaw structures.

BANSHEE BOW

FUNCTION: Ranged bow primarily designed to be used in battle from the back of a banshee

SIZE AND WEIGHT: 2.9 meters, 3.4 kilograms

MATERIALS AND CONSTRUCTION: Composite bow made from horn, decorated with banshee motifs and markings. The handle is made from woven fiber adhered with a plant-based glue. The string is made from gut and decorated with beads. The very light threads on the string can help determine wind direction for a stationary shot. The low hand grip and shorter base of the bow allows for easy change of position while in the saddle. The lower part of the bow stays clear of the banshee. It has its own quiver to hold arrows.

BANSHEE QUEUE HARNESS

- -

FUNCTION: Bridle system to hold Na'vi queue and banshee antenna out of the way of rider and weapons

NA'VI NAME: *Eywa te'* (personal name) *tan'sey mak'ta*

SIZE: Various, depending on size of banshee and rider

MATERIALS AND CONSTRUCTION: Tightly woven tensile fibers, plant sinew, and leather. Constructed over a period of months.

All Na'vi must construct a personalized harness for their banshee after they have bonded. The harness is used to keep the bonding queues in a rearward direction for quick and easy access. The banshee antenna is interlaced with the Na'vi queue, which sheathes the Na'vi antenna, to form a neural bond. The Na'vi and banshee are then able to fly in perfect coordination. The harness is called *"Eywa te'* (personal name) *tan'sey mak'ta*. This translates roughly as "the love of Eywa's embrace is gifted to (the rider's name)" This is an acknowledgment of the beauty of connecting with the consciousness of another living creature such as a banshee or direhorse.

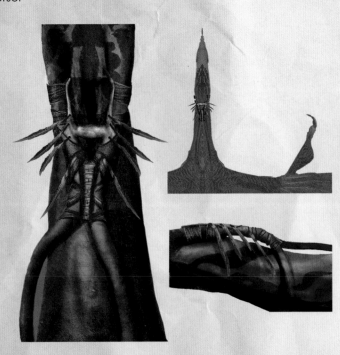

TOY BANSHEE

FUNCTION: Child's plaything

NA'VI NAME: *Su'shiri t'acto sa*

SIZE: Various, but usually no more than 40 centimeters wingspan

WEIGHT: Roughly .5 kilogram

MATERIALS AND CONSTRUCTION: Flexible sticks and twigs woven into the shape of a banshee, decorated with colored twine, twigs, sticks, and reeds

Every Na'vi child has a toy banshee. Most children personalize the toys with their own decorations of twine and shells. The toy serves as a daily reminder that the child will one day bond with a living banshee. Such reminders help the young Na'vi focus on honing their skills, including the mastery of the banshee catcher.

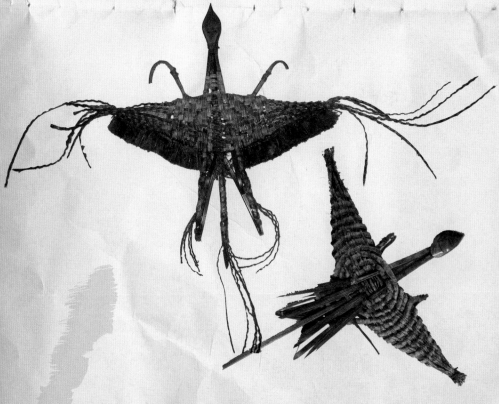

AVATAR 66

FOREST BANSHEE

COMMON NAME: Forest banshee

NA'VI NAME: *Ikranay*

HABITAT: Rainforests, both upper and lower canopy. Rookeries spread throughout cliffs and mesas of mountainous regions.

ANATOMY: Obsidian-like teeth, complex multicolored mottling on translucent wing membranes. Four wings (two aft). Bones comprised of biologically produced carbon fiber composite.

FEEDING ECOLOGY: Aerial predator, carnivore. Usually feeds on smaller rainforest creatures, including stingbat and prolemuris.

SIZE: Wingspan of 7 meters

This smaller cousin to the mountain banshee is also a feared predator. But it lacks the size to support a Na'vi rider.

Forest banshees usually hunt alone, but can migrate in large flocks spread out in a wide, loose pattern (the reason for this behavior is not well understood). Like a Terran reef shark, the forest banshee may size up potential large prey, but seldom attacks anything close to its size, preferring smaller forest animals. A banshee will make an exception, however, in the case of self-defense or when it finds large prey in distress. Then, also like sharks, banshees will congregate to feed, and if necessary will fight one another for their portion.

The creature shares the same basic anatomical advantages as the mountain banshee: strong, carbon fiber bones; specialized flight muscles; and a stiff torso to support its wings. They can make subtle adjustments to their flight attitude and speed with an articulated tail tip, which can flare or remain tucked.

Related to stingbat and mountain banshee. Bioluminescent markings easily spotted from RDA Scorpion gunship during night patrols. Favorite food source for leonopteryx.

Dinicthoid

COMMON NAME: Dinicthoid

TAXONOMY: *Gargoylia macropisceae,* or "giant gargoyle fish"

HABITAT: Pandoran lakes and murky lowland drainages

ANATOMY: Semitransparent body revealing spinal column and inner organs. Heavily armored with triangular, bladelike teeth.

FEEDING ECOLOGY: Voracious predator. Because of fierceness and thick armor comprised of cartilage, it can feed on both smaller and larger fish. Can also feed on plant life, including fallen seeds and pods.

SIZE: Up to 1 meter in length

When hunting at night, the dinicthoid can pulse with bioluminescence to take on the appearance of a smaller, more docile creature to lure prey closer. Conversely, it can control its markings to appear even larger and fiercer.

Its head features two large, protruding red eyes that can see for long distances underwater in dim light. It also features a disconcertingly humanoid false face (used to befuddle or frighten would-be predators) that is created by folds at the top of the skull.

When stimulated by prey or predators, it can reach high speeds by gyrating its flexible sides, much like a manta ray. It also has two flipper fins extruding from either side just beyond the head that are used for propulsion and steering.

Scientists continue to marvel at the ferocity of the fish. Pandoran biologists recently watched as an unlucky young sturmbeest waded into a small pond to drink, only to be dragged beneath the surface by a school of ambitious dinicthy.

Such theatrical violence has led scientists to fear that the fish might be smuggled back to private aquariums on Earth. Should this occur (followed by the inevitable release of the fish into sewers or canals) the consequences for our already-distressed ecosystems would be dire.

Captive specimens are extremely aggressive and have been known to slam against the glass of a holding aquarium. Although dangerous, it is a prized food of the Na'vi, who consider it a sign of courage to confront the fish.

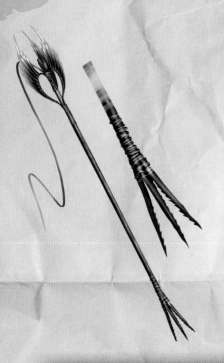

EVIL SPACE FISH! WEAPONIZED, DINICTHOID HAVE BEEN SPOTTED AT RDA RESEARCH AQUARIUMS IN THE GREAT BASIN. RDA CORPORATE CULTURE HAS SHOWN EVIDENCE OF A CERTAIN ACQUISITIVENESS FOR DINICTHOID SPAWNED IN RDA LABS. RDA MIDDLE MANAGEMENT NOW EMPLOY PH-BALANCING POOL TECHNICIANS TO SUSTAIN THE LIFE OF THEIR EVIL SPACE FISH.

FISHING ARROW

FUNCTION: Medium-range fishing weapon

SIZE AND WEIGHT: 1.8 meters, .35 kilograms

MATERIALS AND CONSTRUCTION: Arrowhead made from natural seed case that drops from the canopy and corkscrews itself into the ground, creating a three-pronged head. Fletching is intricately bound feather-like tufts on an arched filament. Barbed wooden spines bound to shaft of arrow.

Broad arrowhead is mostly flat but with slight spiral ridges. String attached to the rear of the arrow prevents the fish from swimming away once arrow is embedded.

DIREHORSE

COMMON NAME: Direhorse

TAXONOMY: *Equidirus hoplites,* or "feared armored horse"

HABITAT: Rainforests and grasslands, but adaptable to most Pandoran environments. A grazing animal that has been domesticated by the Na'vi as a riding animal.

ANATOMY: Horselike creature with six legs, tough plated hide with no fur, long neck and small head, bold stripes, flexible chitinous carbon composite armor over shoulders and along the back of the neck and head

FEEDING ECOLOGY: Land omnivore that uses long snout to feed on sap. Some protein intake through insects trapped in sap. Favored food is direhorse pitcher plant. Effective pollinator.

SIZE: More then 4.25 meters long, up to 4 meters in height

The direhorse has two long, thin antennae that emerge from either side of the top of the skull. These appendages have feathery tips that move constantly (almost like a kind of sea grass) and seek out the antennae of other direhorses as they move near. Biologists believe that the touch of antennae is for pleasure and affection, but also a means of transferring information about food sources and potential dangers; herds often move in unison shortly after touching antennae.

The Na'vi are excellent riders. And the direhorse, with its six legs, is a swift and nimble mount and well adapted to the rugged Pandoran terrain. Many direhorses are tamed to aid in the hunt and battle. To bond with (or, in human terms, to "break") a direhorse, a Na'vi must mount the animal and connect his or her neural queue (or "neural whip") to one of the animal's two antennae. Once queue and antennae touch, the feathery tendrils automatically intertwine, almost as if possessed of free will. Although the exact motive force remains unknown, it is believed that the antennae may secrete a pheromone that evokes the unique intertwining.

Once connected, the Na'vi rider can communicate motor commands instantly through the neural interface. The apparent lack of effort makes it seem as if the direhorse is an extension of the rider's own body. This frees up the Na'vi to use a bow and arrow during a hunt or battle.

Unlike the mountain banshee, however, the neural link made between rider and direhorse does not lead to a lifelong, exclusive bond between Na'vi and animal; although, Na'vi have their favorite mounts, it is possible and permissible to ride another clan member's direhorse.

The direhorse is a perfect mount to ride in the obstacle-strewn close quarters of a Pandoran forest; they can turn on a dime, have excellent reaction times, and can leap large distances.

When wild, the animals move together in a loose herd through the forests, feeding on tree bark and shrubs. Herds numbering in the dozens have been spotted from aircraft. But evidence (including scatological and plant impact) suggests that herds of more than one hundred animals are not uncommon.

The animals are easily startled and, when all six legs are working in unison, can reach ninety-five kilometers per hour. The direhorse is larger by a third than the largest Terran draft horses, such as the Clydesdale or the Percheron, and substantially larger than the biggest horse ever recorded on Earth.

Animal has neural interface that allows Na'vi and direhorse to move together with apparent effortlessness. A highly intelligent, calm creature that, like the Na'vi, can turn fierce in the face of battle.

DIREHORSE LEADS

FUNCTION: Leading direhorse while dismounted

NA'VI NAME: *Na'hla buk'ne,* or "face pull"

SIZE AND WEIGHT: Varies, but roughly 60 centimeters, 1 kilogram

MATERIALS AND CONSTRUCTION: Made from various strong tensile fibers, plant sinew, animal leather. Elements woven into design that is both functional and ceremonial.

Various different styles of leads and their distinct woven decorations have been handed down by tradition. The lead is slipped loosely over the front of a direhorse's head. Unlike Terran bridles, these are not used for steering the direhorse while riding. Na'vi riders do not manually steer their horses, but rely instead on the neural link between animal and rider provided by their queues. This lead is used when the rider has disconnected his or her queue and is walking the animal from one place to another.

DIREHORSE BOW

FUNCTION: Ranged bow for use while riding direhorse

SIZE AND WEIGHT: 3 meters, roughly 3.6 kilograms

MATERIALS AND CONSTRUCTION: Bow is made from shaped wood. Handle made from scaled animal skin adhered with a plant-based glue and additionally bound with decorative woven banding. The string is made from sturmbeest gut. Low hand grip and shorter base of the bow allows for easy change of position while in the saddle.

After completion of Iknimaya and Uniltaron, each hunter is allowed to carve a bow from a branch of Hometree. These bows are a symbol of adulthood and its accompanying responsibilities. They also serve as the primary hunting weapon for a Na'vi. This ranged bow is highly decorated and appropriate for use in ceremonies. But it is crafted to the peak of Na'vi design and functions extremely well in real-life situations.

FAN LIZARD

COMMON NAME: Fan Lizard

TAXONOMY: *Fanisaurus pennatus,* or "winged fan lizard"

HABITAT: Rainforest, with a preference for large ferns

ANATOMY: Spinelike structure that unfurls into a magenta and purple bioluminescent membrane

FEEDING ECOLOGY: Nocturnal land omnivore that feeds on tree sap and small insects. Often feeds in swarms.

SIZE: 45 centimeters long in folded position, roughly 1 meter across when unfurled

At first glance, this unique lizard appears to be little more than a dull, ruler-length reptile with few apparent virtues. When agitated, however, it unfurls like an antique Chinese fan and spins away to safety. In an instant, it morphs from pitiful to beautiful and then, just as rapidly, is once again a rather common-looking lizard.

Understandably, the fan lizard is a favorite among young Na'vi who cherish this natural spectacle. At every opportunity, a Na'vi child will run through a field of ferns to disturb a group of resting fan lizards, and then marvel as the luminous magenta and purple discs float to the safety of a nearby branch. In the Pandoran twilight, this shimmering flight is strangely alien even to the Na'vi.

An ancient dance (usually performed by children) celebrates the lizard. Two dancers stand side by side to create a rigid "spine." Another group of children run by and taunt the pair, at which point the entwined dancers "unfurl" into a circular shape and "float" in a zig-zag pattern through the other dancers. This dance is usually accompanied by *hufwe,* or wind instruments.

Given Pandoran gravity and air density, the rapid opening of the lizard produces enough angular momentum to create lift, which startles predators and removes the fan lizard from danger in one move.

ONE OF GRACE AUGUSTINE'S FAVORITE ANIMALS ON PANDORA.

Great Leonopteryx

COMMON NAME: Leonopteryx

NA'VI NAME: *Toruk,* or "last shadow"

TAXONOMY: *Leonopteryx rex,* or "flying king lion"

HABITAT: Mountain aeries and skies above the Pandoran rainforest

ANATOMY: Closely related to the banshee, although significantly larger. Striped scarlet, yellow, and black, with a midnight blue head. Sharp crest on head can be used to injure or disembowel prey, or cut vegetation obstructing flight. Distensible jaw, large brain cavity. Membranous wings are stretched taut over carbon fiber bone structure. Powerful talons for grasping prey and perching. Twin tail for flight control. Flow-through ventilation for high performance.

FEEDING ECOLOGY: Apex aerial predator. Carnivore. Main food source is forest and mountain banshees, occasional medusa. Can also feed under the rainforest canopy on ground animals such as hexapede. No known threat from other creatures. Solo hunter.

SIZE: Wingspan is more than 25 meters

The fierce beauty and nobility of the leonopteryx give it a central place in Na'vi lore and culture. It is celebrated in dance, song, and with elaborate totems that symbolize both the fear and respect accorded to the creature. Indeed, the leonopteryx is crucial to the Na'vi's sense of destiny and interconnectedness.

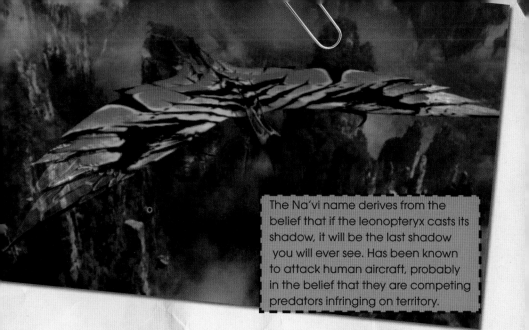

The Na'vi name derives from the belief that if the leonopteryx casts its shadow, it will be the last shadow you will ever see. Has been known to attack human aircraft, probably in the belief that they are competing predators infringing on territory.

The few humans lucky enough to have survived seeing this creature have also marveled at its iridescent grace and command of the Pandoran skies.

The leonopteryx shares the basic body plan of the forest and mountain banshees: grasping claws, long teeth for snatching prey on the fly, flexible wings for maneuverability, excellent eyesight with forward binocular vision, and high intelligence. Its powerful jaws, which can open to a wide angle, are efficient enough to cleave a mountain banshee in midflight. The leonopteryx also has an impressive rate of climb and, when it plummets out of the sky, resembles a massive Terran hawk.

The wings of the leonopteryx are composed of individual finned members that can separate to act as a slotted airfoil, or overlap and seal to form a solid surface. When separated, they can rotate individually to induce or retard vortex formation. These finned members are not unlike the primary feathers of a Terran bird. As with many Pandoran creatures, their fiber composite bones help the massive animal achieve flight through the dense Pandoran atmosphere.

Leonopteryx rookeries are difficult to locate, although some have been sited in the Hallelujah Mountains. This species mates for life and breeds only once every two years. They travel singly or in pairs and have never been observed to swarm. They are normally wary of others of their kind, and rightly so; an aerial battle between two leonopteryx that lasted over three hours was observed by a team of avatars. The battle ended when both great beasts fell to the ground, mortally wounded. Based on the distinct yelps, the avatars believed that the wounded leonopteryx were dispatched by a large pack of viperwolves.

HAMMERHEAD TITANOTHERE

COMMON NAME: Hammerhead

TAXONOMY: *Titanotheris hammercephalis,* or "four-eyed titanothere"

HABITAT: Prefers open grasslands, but frequent visitor to rainforests

ANATOMY: Massive, low-slung head with bony projections on either side of the skull similar to Terran hammerhead shark. Soft ungulate mouth is protected by a rigid, beaklike jaw structure.

FEEDING ECOLOGY: Land herbivore. Main food sources are grass and shrubs, but also eats various fruits and leaves of the rainforest.

SIZE: Can be 6 meters in height, 11 meters long

A plant eater, but potentially deadly. Nearly twice the size of an African elephant, but much faster.

This massive, grazing creature travels in small herds or packs. It is moderately social, but also extremely territorial and hierarchical. Constant threat displays, both visible and audible, are a large part of the titanothere's day. When angered (which happens easily and often), a titanothere will lower its head and charge at the perceived threat. The sheer momentum and ferocity of this display is usually enough to send any Pandoran creature running for cover.

Titanotheres also possess a brightly colored threat display crest with rigid, chitinous backings that can be raised when confronted by an adversary. Both the hammerhead structure and the colored skin fan are also used to attract and compete for females during the mating season.

The imposing hammerhead structure is formed of cartilage rather than bone in the juvenile animal. It can bend to allow the animal to pass through restricted spaces that an inexperienced young hammerhead might enter. As it matures, the structure ossifies and becomes solid bone. Fighting males will attempt to injure their opponents' eyes with the knobs at the ends of their hammers. The titanothere is highly territorial. Alpha males use their considerable momentum to mark their territory by smashing trees, thus warning other animals (including titanothere bulls) to steer clear.

The titanothere has poor distance vision, but makes up for this with acute hearing and an excellent sense of smell. Although massive, its six limbs allow it to pivot rapidly when it detects a threat from the side or rear. The animal's overlapping body plates and large, bony shoulder and back offer protection during battles with other titanothere or large creatures such as the leonopteryx or thanator.

HELLFIRE WASP

COMMON NAME: Hellfire wasp

TAXONOMY: *Magnivespa velox*, or "fast large wasp"

HABITAT: Various wasp species have been found in most Pandoran microclimates, including mountain valleys, streambeds, and beaches. *Magnivespa velox* lives in rainforest and swampland and prefers to build small nests in fallen, rotting trees.

ANATOMY: Hard exoskeleton, compound eyes, bioluminescence, dual stinger

FEEDING ECOLOGY: Most adults feed on sap, fruit, and carrion, and provide paralyzed insects to their young

SIZE: Wingspan of 13 centimeters

The hellfire wasp is shaped much like a typical Earth wasp, but is similar in size to a sparrow. Although usually observed flying alone, swarms nearly the size of a robodozer have been sighted.

It has an accurate organic targeting system that uses an olfactory organ to detect the biochemistry of any nearby creature. If it senses danger, its flight becomes agitated and erratic and it will usually attack.

Although humans have not yet been killed by a hellfire wasp, it is common for RDA personnel to be placed on medical leave for several days because of a sting. It is believed, however, that a swarm of the wasps will eventually cause a fatality.

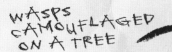

WASPS CAMOUFLAGED ON A TREE

Bioluminescence makes them highly visible at night, but they are still fast enough to strike even with advanced warning. Sting is excruciating, but rarely lethal to humans or Na'vi unless attacked by swarm.

THE RDA WILL TELL YOU THAT CORPORATE SOLDIERS ARE SO WELL OUTFITTED THAT THEY CAN SUBDUE ANYTHING AND EVERYTHING ON PANDORA. EMPHATICALLY NOT TRUE. SOMETHING THAT SHOULD GIVE YOU HOPE. ACCORDING TO SOURCES ON THE MOON, WASPS OF THE HELLFIRE VARIETY HAVE ATTACKED AND KILLED MERCENARIES.

HEXAPEDE

COMMON NAME: Hexapede

NA'VI NAME: *Yerik*

TAXONOMY: *Sexcruscervus caeruleus,* or "blue six-legged deer"

HABITAT: Ubiquitous in various biomes of Pandora, including rainforest, savanna, subarctic tundra, and mountainous regions

ANATOMY: Small, sloped skull is topped by a light-colored fan structure. Eyes are wide-spaced and large. Longish snout that ends in a small bifurcating jaw. Bifurcated lip that can be retracted. Twin horn structures that sheathe a thin, patterned membrane. Skin membrane "beard" hangs under jaw and runs length of neck. Twin lines of dark hairlike bristles run down its back. Long, thin neck and legs ending in round, beveled hooves. Body is dark blue with white-yellow stripes.

FEEDING ECOLOGY: Land herbivore

SIZE: Up to 1.5 meters long, 2 meters in height

One of the most beautiful and fragile creatures on Pandora, the hexapede is a prime target for any land or aerial predator. The rapid pace of their breeding is the only strategy that keeps them from being culled out of the Pandoran ecology.

Along with the sturmbeest, the hexapede is one of the key animals responsible for the survival of the Na'vi. Its image is represented on the war banners of several clans, and the animal is often depicted on shields and in carvings. Its leather is used in a myriad of ways, from musical instruments to clothing.

These docile creatures appear to have little hostility either among their own herd or in the presence of a predator. They are only moderately fast runners, although they can weave, bob, and turn with the best prey. The latter helps them survive in the grasslands, but when they venture into the forest for the food they crave (including tree bark and various leaves and berries) this strategy has less effectiveness, since they have less maneuvering room.

The hexapede's twin horn structures sheathe a thin, patterned membrane. The horns can pivot and pull taut the membrane for a large threat display. It is believed that this membrane may also act to amplify the sound of nearby predators. In addition, the hexapede also has feathery scent organs on both sides of its head. These organs sample the air as an early warning system to alert the animal to the presence of a predator.

> By tradition, the first animal that a prospective warrior is allowed to kill when making the rite of passage from child to adult.

PANDORAN ARTIFACTS, INCLUDING THE MUCH-PRIZED CEREMONIAL BATTLE SHIELD ADORNED WITH THE IMAGE OF THE HEXAPEDE, ARE A PROFITABLE SIDELINE FOR THE RDA. HUGELY EXPENSIVE AND ONLY AFFORDABLE BY THE VERY FEW, THEY ARE COLLECTED BY THE RDA AND ASSOCIATED INDIVIDUALS AND GROUPS. TREAT ANYONE WHO COLLECTS PANDORAN ARTIFACTS WITH GREAT SUSPICION.

SHIELDS

FUNCTION: Personal protection during hunt, battle. Also ceremonial use during dances, other rituals.

NA'VI NAME: *M'resh'tuyu*

SIZE AND WEIGHT: Various

MATERIALS AND CONSTRUCTION: Wood structure held together with highly decorative woven materials. Materials include animal skin (including hexapede), plant fibers, twine, shells, and wood.

Although the shields are effective as protection, their ceremonial use has become more and more important as battles between Na'vi clans have become mostly a thing of the past. All shields are highly decorated. But ceremonial shields are woven with traditional patterns that depict a story from Na'vi history. The patterns and construction are based on centuries of visual tradition and visual language. The image of the fleet hexapede is common. Many symbols are abstract images of the protective power of Eywa, or of heroic ancestors. Newer shields depict images of Terran gunships (or *kunsip* to the Na'vi) and AMP Suits.

HUNTING ARROWS

FUNCTION: Arrow used for hunting

SIZE AND WEIGHT: Various, from 1. 5 to 2.5

MATERIALS: Plant gum (or resin) arrowhead bound to wooden arrow shaft. On longer arrows, the arrowhead is mostly flat but with slight spiral ridges made from a natural seed case that drops from the canopy.

DESCRIPTION: Ranged weapon, relatively short so that they can be maneuvered in a jungle environment. Na'vi weapons have changed little over the course of eons.

MEDUSA-AEROCOELENTERATES

COMMON NAME: Medusa

NA'VI NAME: *Lonataya*

TAXONOMY: *Aerocnidaria aerae,* or "aerial jellyfish"

HABITAT: Sky above mountainous regions of Pandora

ANATOMY: Clear membranous sac with attached tentacles

FEEDING ECOLOGY: Aerial carnivore that feeds on small, rodentlike animals on forest floor and, occasionally, on creatures as large as a hexapede, Slinger, or even humanoid. Can also pluck prolemuris and roosting tetrapterons from forest canopy.

SIZE: Bell is up to 15 meters in diameter. Tentacles can reach more than 35 meters.

Drifting over the mountaintops of Pandora, these deadly and beautiful creatures look like the alien offspring of a Portuguese man-of-war and a adblimp. During mating season, regions of the southern continent of Australis are blackened by the shadow of the medusa swarm as it swirls in a dance of interlocking tentacles.

The medusa's clear membranous sac, or "bell," is filled with hydrogen gas produced by the digestion of its prey. This gas allows the medusa to float above the canopy in search of potential victims.

Their translucent tentacles, which create a kind of curtain sweeping across the terrain, make a faint swishing sound that causes animals to scurry. The tentacles, which are three to eight centimeters in diameter, are replete with sensors that react instantly to the touch of an animal by curling into a viselike grip. The tentacles are also lined with electrocytes that can channel a current from an organ in the bell that produces electricity. The shock can be strong enough to stun a banshee or kill a full-grown human. Once in the grip of the tough, leathery appendages, it is unlikely that any creature will survive. The tentacles then lift the prey to the medusa's pulpy mouth.

As a defense mechanism, the bell can pulse (much like an octopus) to give some directional control. It expels gas to descend and uses fluids from trim bladders to rise. For the most part, however, the creature is content to drift on the winds and hunt opportunistically.

Their eyes (or, more accurately, their optical sensors) are in a fleshy belt around the bottom of the bell. They provide the animal with a 360-degree view of the terrain beneath them. To look up, they must use extraordinary effort to reorient themselves.

Given their limited mobility, they could become easy prey for other aerial predators, such as stingbats and banshees. But the medusa has little edible flesh. In addition, the unpleasant and potentially dangerous release of hydrogen gas is a natural deterrent to any predator; when the bell is punctured by tooth or claw, the medusa has been observed flying in erratic circles like a punctured balloon, confusing or startling the predator. For these reasons, they are rarely attacked. Its only consistent enemy is the great leonopteryx, which, if deprived of food, will on occasion attack and eat the foul-tasting medusa.

Aerial battle between *ikran* and *Ionataya* is considered to be one of the great natural spectacles on Pandora.

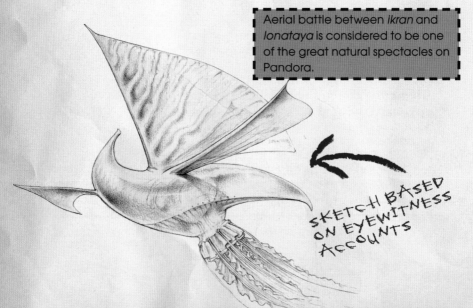

SKETCH BASED ON EYEWITNESS ACCOUNTS

PROLEMURIS

COMMON NAME: Prolemuris

TAXONOMY: *Prolemuris noctis*, or "night squirrel"

HABITAT: Rainforest canopy

ANATOMY: Large, binocular-like eyes, apelike skull with fleshy snout. Small nostrils and jaw. Teeth are needle sharp. Membranous wing flaps. Split top lip.

FEEDING ECOLOGY: Arboreal herbivore. Teeth adapted to cut through tensile strength of Pandoran flora. Known to eat insects on occasion. Predators include banshees, viperwolves.

SIZE: Can reach up to 1 meter in height

This chattering, unaggressive tree dweller prefers the relative safety of the canopy to the dangers of the rainforest floor.

The prolemuris has lateral membranes that grow out of its sides and between its lower arm and thigh. When it leaps from tree to tree, the wind catches in the flaps and slows the animal's rate of fall. This allows the animal to fall for more than twelve meters without risk of injury. They have hollow bones, and the density of their musculature and flesh is also porous, which makes them much lighter than they appear (even the largest weigh less than six kilograms).

The prolemuris can use its four arms to move through the trees faster than an average man can run. It has near-perfect balance and its superb depth perception allows it to leap from branch to branch while selecting just the right handhold out of the forest mosaic (in this it resembles the Na'vi, who can also move through the rainforest canopy with tremendous agility).

Its ears are long, drooping flaps that can move independently of one another in order to track sounds in a precise stereo field. Its toes are webbed and have a vestigial thumb nub that helps the animal cling to branches. It has two arms that bifurcate into four forearms;

the upper bones of the arms have fused, enabling mobility as they navigate through the trees. (Biologists believe that this may be an evolutionary precursor to the two-armed Na'vi). One digit is a four-jointed finger topped with a humanlike fingernail, the other is a two-jointed thumb that is adapted for clasping tree limbs and vines.

They dwell in the trees in large tribal groups, and although there are some violent intertribal contests to establish hierarchy, there is little battle between tribes. They are highly social, although they do not care for their young as avidly or carefully as Terran chimpanzees. Still, the prolemuris is a diligent and effective breeder, with the female achieving reproductive readiness three times a year.

The mating habits of the prolemuris are similar to some species of Terran apes, including the now-extinct gorilla, hamadryas baboon, and howler monkey (along with several human cultures as well). An alpha male prolemuris will mate with several females concurrently and assist with the rearing of each offspring. But this polygynous arrangement is by no means an indication of male dominance; it is believed that prolemuris social structure is largely matriarchal, with the female clearly in charge of the mate selection process.

THE EXPRESSIVE JOY WITH WHICH THE PROLEMURIS MOVES THROUGH PANDORA'S DENSE FOLIAGE IS AERIAL POETRY. WE SHOULD REVEL IN THOSE MOMENTS OF HIJACKED BEAUTY, EVEN IF PACKAGED AND DELIVERED BY RDA MEDIA.

Offal of the prolemuris is considered a delicacy among some Na'vi clans and is used in food wraps.

Slinger

Common Name: Slinger

Na'vi Name: *Lenay'ga*

Taxonomy: *Acediacutus xenoterribili* or "strange terrible sloth"

Habitat: Rainforest

Anatomy: Muscular neck, triangular detachable head with stinger and neurotoxic venom glands

Feeding Ecology: Land predator, carnivore. Hexapede is a staple food.

Size: 2.4 meters in height

This slothlike animal is one of the oddest and most dangerous creatures yet discovered on Pandora.

When hunting, this creature moves slowly and silently through the forest ferns. When it senses prey, its muscular neck cocks back into a striking position, then snaps forward. Its long, pointed, and winged head detaches and flies toward the prey as a self-guiding venomous projectile. After the head embeds itself into its target (often a hexapede), the dart emits a series of high-pitched squeals. The signals allow the body (now sightless) to home in, locate, and move toward the detached part. Still separated, the strange partners enjoy their prey. Sated, the neck bends down and a mesh of hairlike tendrils rejoins head with body.

As if this were not compelling enough, biologists were stunned to discover that the body and its dartlike head are not a single creature with a singular method of hunting. Instead, the dart is actually the "child" of the body and will stay in the symbiotic relationship with its "mother" until it is too big to fly. It then mates, detaches from the mother-body and metamorphoses into a smaller, complete slinger with its own offspring dart-head. Left behind without its dart offspring, the mother-body is unable to feed itself and dies. In this odd cycle of renewal, each generation becomes the brain for the previous generation.

This would all be academically intriguing were it not for the fact that slingers have proven deadly to human colonists. Several have died—badly—after being struck by a slinger dart.

Na'vi hunters have been known to retrieve a dart that has been orphaned from its mother-body to use later as an effective weapon.

> Na'vis rub on sap from a leaf that replicates the smell of a slinger to ward off attacks by viperwolves.

STINGBAT

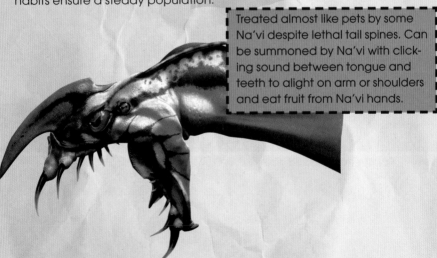

COMMON NAME: Stingbat

NA'VI NAME: *Riti*

TAXONOMY: *Scorpiobattus volansii,* or "flying scorpion bat"

HABITAT: Rainforest canopy

ANATOMY: Translucent fangs and claws, bioluminescence on periphery of wing membrane and torso. Scorpion-like tail stinger. Small brain cavity. Four eyes.

FEEDING ECOLOGY: Nocturnal aerial predator, omnivore. Feeds mostly from canopy on rodent-sized creatures, lizards, and fruit. Usually solo feeders, but will swarm against larger prey such as small hexapede.

SIZE: Wingspan of 1.2 meters.

This foul-tempered aerial predator has a highly developed visual navigation system. Yet despite this organic "intelligence," their small brain cavity and cerebral cortex inhibits their innate survival mechanisms. Despite a constant slaughter, the creatures continue to fly into the range of automated sentry guns that defend the Hell's Gate compound.

Their diminished cerebral capacity makes them common prey for larger predators such as banshees. But their prodigious mating habits ensure a steady population.

Treated almost like pets by some Na'vi despite lethal tail spines. Can be summoned by Na'vi with clicking sound between tongue and teeth to alight on arm or shoulders and eat fruit from Na'vi hands.

Sturmbeest

COMMON NAME: Sturmbeest

NA'VI NAME: *Talioang*

TAXONOMY: *Bovindicum monocerii,* or "horned blue cow"

HABITAT: Migratory animal that dwells in wetlands and river deltas

ANATOMY: Massive buffalo-like herd beast with six legs and indigo and orange coloring. Its skull features a single large bony hornlike extrusion above the eyes. Extrusions are reddish or orange, with striated slashes of blue.

FEEDING ECOLOGY: Land animal that feeds on grass, shrubs, and various fungi. Hornlike jaw extension acts as plow for digging up roots, grubs, and other subsurface food.

SIZE: Average animal is 6 meters long, up to 4.5 meters in height. Weighs roughly 900 kilograms.

The sturmbeest is one of the main sources of animal products for the Na'vi. As such, sturmbeest are a primary organizing force in clan culture. A number of different clans extol the virtues of the animal in textiles, music, song, dance, and art.

Sturmbeest are herd animals. They are extremely social and highly protective of their young. They are also territorial and will mass for attack against any would-be predator. When the predator is too large or in too great a number, they will stampede, often breaking off into smaller packs for evasion.

The male is usually about 15 percent larger than the female, and has a bigger ridge bone on its back. The male also has a dramatic top horn that is used for defense and in mating contests against other bulls.

Their brain-mass-to-body-weight ratio is low, and the creatures are slow to react and slow to stop reacting. The young, old, and lame are prey only to the largest or fiercest predators, such as viperwolf packs, the thanator, and occasionally a large leonopteryx.

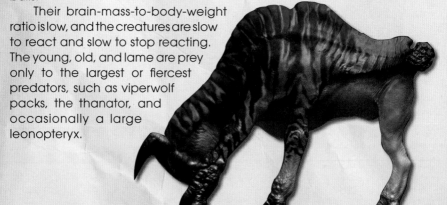

Poor long-distance vision. But hearing is acute and their sense of smell extends over long distances. They have been observed being startled by a predator more than 3 kilometers upwind.

ONE OF OUR PEOPLE ON PANDORA SAYS THAT A STURMBEEST STAMPEDE IS "AS LOUD AS A VALKYRIE LIFTOFF." HASN'T BEEN A SOUND LIKE THAT ON EARTH SINCE THE DEMISE OF THE AMERICAN BISON.

HUNT SONGS

FUNCTION: Ritual and social singing

NA'VI NAME: *Taron tìrol*

PERFORMANCE STYLE: Rhythmic group chanting while on the hunt or during puberty rituals. Unison singing for social dances, especially in conjunction with prehunt rituals. Usually accompanied by different sizes of sturmbeest gongs or various drums.

Songs for Uniltaron have a strong driving rhythm and wild, ecstatic style. Sung by adult Na'vi who have attained *Tsahaylu* with their banshee, during Uniltaron, or during puberty rituals prior to first attempt at *Iknimaya*.

Hunt songs are often used to accompany rites of passage, including a precursor to the moment when a Na'vi first bonds with his or her banshee. They may be sung in unison, but more often are chanted breathlessly. During Uniltaron, in which Na'vi seek their spirit animal during a chemically induced trance, they express themselves musically as the spirit moves.

Other hunt songs focus on hunting activities, extolling the strength of both hunter and hunted, praying for the worthiness of the hunter, speaking to the spirits of the forest creatures, etc. These may be sung in many contexts: before or during a hunt, prior to battle with external forces, and during social events.

Many of the songs for puberty rituals and hunting are performed as nonmelodic group chanting in a very forceful, rhythmic grunting style. In this style, the glottal stops and ejective consonants inherent in the Na'vi language are emphasized. (See lyrics on page 99.) It is believed that this chanting or grunting style is the oldest extant Na'vi expressive style, because of the way the song style incorporates and emphasizes these linguistic elements.

During some rituals, members of the clan will perform agile "hand-dancing" in which their long, tendril-like fingers weave a deeply symbolic and poetic narrative. Rapid, controlled shifts of the dancers' bioluminescent spots often add to the magical beauty of the performance.

Uniltaron, or Dream Hunt, songs are especially interesting. While under the chemically induced effects that mark the Dream Hunt, a Na'vi may utilize any kind of expression: standard social song structures, imitations of domestic cascading vocal style or children's songs from deep in their memories, wildly improvised songs, or chants. The only type of songs not heard in this context are personal songs or the ritual songs of mourning.

Here is a typical example of hunt song lyrics, which often display great respect for the potential prey:

HUNT SONG

We are walking your way	*Terìran ayoe ayngane*
We are coming	*Zera'u*
We are singing your way	*Rerol ayoe ayngane*
So choose	*Ha ftxey*
Choose one among you	*Awpot set ftxey ayngal a l(u)*
	ayngakip
Who will feed the People.	*Awpot a Na'viru yomtìyìng.*
Chorus (repeated)	
Let my arrow strike true	*Oeyä swizaw nìngay tivakuk*
Let my spear strike the heart	*Oeyä tukrul txe'lanit tivakuk*
Let the truth strike my heart	*Oeri tìngayìl txe'lanit tivakuk*
Let my heart be true.	*Oeyä txe'lan livu ngay.*
You are fast and strong	*Lu nga win sì txur*
You are wise	*Lu nga txantslusam*
I must be fast and strong	*Livu win sì txur oe zene*
So only	*Ha n(ì)'aw*
Only if I am worthy of you	*Pxan livu txo nì'aw oe ngari*
Will you feed the People.	*Tsakrr nga Na'viru yomtìyìng.*
Chorus (repeated)	

TEYLU

NA'VI NAME: *Teylu*

HABITAT: Moist, decomposing trees and vegetation

ANATOMY: Grub, larval stage of Pandoran centipede-like insect. Opaque skin revealing skein of veins, cartilage.

FEEDING ECOLOGY: Feeds on decayed vegetive matter, moss, smaller insects

SIZE: Up to 8 centimeters, usually smaller

A main source of protein for the Na'vi, along with sturmbeest and hexapede. Similar to a jumbo shrimp, slightly sweet. Usually steamed, but Na'vi also cook them with vegetables over open fire on a stick, similar to Terran shish kebab.

LIKE THE MASSIVE TILAPIA FARMS OF THE LAST CENTURY, TEYLU HARVESTING HAS THE POTENTIAL TO BECOME A PRODUCTIVE FOOD SOURCE. TEYLU ARE LIKE THE MAGGOTS NOW RIFE ON EARTH AND PRIZED AS SNACKS, FRIED AND SALTY. THE TASTY TEYLU HAVE A HIGHER PROTEIN CONTENT, HOWEVER, AND BREED MORE RAPIDLY IN WASTE. AS EASY TO RAISE AS WORMS AND MORE PALATABLE.

THANATOR

COMMON NAME: Thanator

NA'VI NAME: *Palulukan,* or "dry mouth bringer of Fear"

TAXONOMY: *Thanatora ferox,* or "fierce thanator"

HABITAT: Rainforest floor. Similar species have been observed in subarctic regions.

ANATOMY: Armored head and massive distensible armored jaw. Teeth are twenty-three centimeters long. Burnished black skin banded with stripes of yellow and scarlet. Ten external sensory quills. Upper lips fold back for maximum tooth extension. Armored by chitinous plating over dorsal area.

FEEDING ECOLOGY: Apex land predator, omnivore with preference for nocturnal hunting

SIZE: Reaches over 5.5 meters long, more than 2.5 meters in height.

Although many regions of the moon have yet to be explored, biologists currently believe that the thanator may be the apex land predator on Pandora. Reminiscent of a Terran panther, this enormous, powerful animal is unique in its ability to lord over its territory and strike fear into the largest and fiercest of Pandora's creatures. Even the Na'vi, who are renowned for their courage, are shaken by the approach of the creature; it is not celebrated in dance or song.

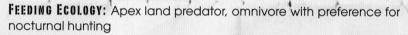

Its musculature is pronounced and impressive, providing power for protracted runs and leaps. The speed of its neck and jaw strike is as swift as a camera shutter. In addition to conventional ripping and tearing, the thanator can also deliver a lethal blow from its armored tail. The thanator's senses are so highly developed that, depending on atmospheric conditions, it can detect prey up to thirteen kilometers away.

The thanator appears to hunt alone and normally does not stray outside of its territory, which is believed to be roughly three hundred square kilometers. It appears to hunt mainly at night, although seems to make an exception if hungry enough.

Surprisingly, the thanator has ten sensory quills, two each sprouting from armor plating that encircles the rear of the skull. The function of the quills is poorly understood, but it has been hypothesized that they may be tied to an internal mechanism of prey location.

The most fearsome of all Pandoran land predators. Wide, armored tail can slam prey or defend against other thanators. Cartilaginous plates around its neck that can flare, possibly as a threat display but more likely as an echolocation or other sensory pinpointing system. Vulnerable to human and Na'vi weaponry at respiratory exhaust vent. Given its anatomy, it is likely that the thanator is an evolutionary relative to the viperwolf.

VIPERWOLF

COMMON NAME: Viperwolf

NA'VI NAME: *Nantang*

TAXONOMY: *Caniferratus costatus,* or "striped armored wolf"

HABITAT: Rainforest, savanna, subarctic

ANATOMY: Six legs. Mostly black but banded with vermillion and iridescent blue. Burnished, hairless skin. Low-slung head with chitinous armor around neck. Amphipod plating on the back of the neck and spine. Bioluminescence for pack identification. Distensible, snakelike jaw with obsidian teeth. Paddlelike tail used for stability. Leathery paws have opposable thumbs. Shows characteristics of canid on evolutionary path to simian.

FEEDING ECOLOGY: Mostly nocturnal carnivore, highly strategic pack hunter with territories ranging more than 480 square kilometers. Unique coyote-like yelps and snakelike hissing thought to convey hunting information.

SIZE: More than 2 meters long, more than 1 meter in height

With six legs and a lean, powerful torso, the viperwolf has evolved to travel swiftly over long distances in search of prey. The ratio of brain mass to body weight of the average adult viperwolf indicates a high order of mental processing, pattern recognition, and communication skills.

Their keen, intelligent green eyes can see as clearly at night as in the day. Their long-distance vision is only moderate, but their depth perception is superb. Their sense of smell is second only to the thanator (based on the few creatures who have been measured to date). It is believed that a viperwolf can sense prey from more than eight kilometers away.

Very few predators (the mountain banshee among them) will attempt an attack on a viperwolf, who nearly always moves in a pack that can mass into a highly cooperative hunting party within seconds. The pack appears to communicate information about the potential prey or predator with facial ticks, paw gestures, and audio cues.

The viperwolf hunts in small groups, communicating with short coyote-like barks and yelps. Its primatelike paws (which include opposable thumbs) allow it to climb trees as well as to stalk from the ground, thereby creating a three-dimensional "hunting field." When stalking prey, the viperwolf is able to reduce its profile by hugging the ground or clinging to tree limbs. Thus hidden, a viperwolf can often approach within a few meters of unsuspecting prey, and then attack with frightening efficiency. (One biologist describes this graceful but ominous movement as "liquid darkness.")

Only months after birth, a viperwolf cub is required to hunt on its own. However, the cubs mature swiftly and grow to half their adult size by their sixth month. By then, they also have a full set of teeth and their jaw muscles are almost mature; a viperwolf's jaws can exert four kilograms of pressure per square centimeter, easily enough to crush bone, or even stone.

> Humanlike grip allows viperwolves to hunt in rainforest canopy as well as on ground. Animal is revered by the Na'vi for fierce intelligence, devotion to the pack, and strong familial bond.

VIPERWOLF
CUB

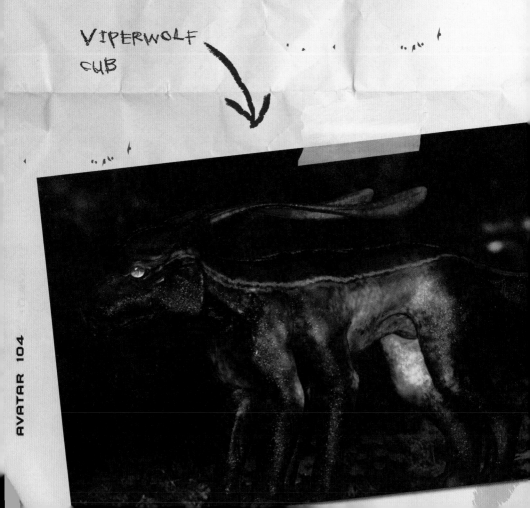

BOLAS

FUNCTION: Entanglement weapon for hunting

SIZE AND WEIGHT: Usually more than 1 meter, roughly 1 kilogram

MATERIALS AND CONSTRUCTION: Bolas weights are made from very hard polished seeds of a slightly concave shape; they stack lightly in a woven pouch, with Hometree motif, made from plant fiber. Bola string is wound around the inner edge.

Mastery of the bolas, which involves accurately flinging the weighted rope for up to ten meters, is an integral part of Na'vi life. Children begin to practice the skill at a young age, years before they join in actual hunts. The bola is a simple weapon that, in the right hands, can drop a sturmbeest at full gallop. It is used to ensnare prey and as a defense against attacking animals. The Na'vi employ this weapon when they want to ensnare an animal rather than kill it outright (viperwolves, for example, will be restrained whenever possible, even if they are attacking). The bolas have hooks that catch on the rope after wrapping around the animal.

STREAMERS

FUNCTION: Visual identification of various Na'vi clans, both for ceremonial and practical purposes

NA'VI NAME: *U'imi*

SIZE AND WEIGHT: Various

MATERIALS AND CONSTRUCTION: Highly decorated animal skins attached to wooden frames. Can also be attached to the harness of direhorses and banshees.

Like the banners and flags of Earth, Na'vi streamers are used for both identification and clan pride, and also as a rallying point during battles. The intricate images that decorate the streamers indicate the clan's name. These images can act as a symbol of inspiration in times of crisis. The images reflect a clan's organizing theme, or special point of pride. The *U'imi huyuticaya*, for example, are known for their tremendous love and respect for viperwolves.

4 FLORA OF PANDORA

Plant life on Pandora is strange and even fantastic. Yet some plants on Pandora bear a striking resemblance to plants on Earth. The diversity of plant life and its range of size and complexity suggest that, as on Earth, the environment on Pandora acts as a strong force for natural selection. The environmental factors that plants experience on Earth—radiation, water, atmospheric gases, and gravity—are present on Pandora, as well, although their characteristics differ profoundly, as the resulting plant life shows. The atmosphere on Pandora is thicker than on Earth, with higher concentrations of carbon dioxide as well as elevated levels of hydrogen sulfide and xenon. Gravity is weaker, while the satellite's magnetic field is incredibly strong. All of these factors have determined the evolution of plant life on Pandora.

As on Earth, plants on Pandora have evolved the ability to respond to gravity, though its force is weaker on Pandora. As a result, gigantism is found in plants, and the typical orientation—stems growing up and roots growing down—does not necessarily hold true. The tallest trees, which are limited on Earth by the physical height to which their transport tissue can move water, reach much greater heights on Pandora in its lower gravity. The presence of a magnetic field and ionizing radiation have selected for growth responses toward these stimuli, named magnetotropism and radiotropism, respectively. Similarly, some plants are magnetonastic, meaning they move in response to the magnetic field on Pandora. These unique responses make the more typical touch response, thigmotropism, which is found on both Earth and Pandora, seem quite tame by comparison.

Although plants on Pandora have been given various common and Latin names, using the standard nomenclature accepted on Earth for biological organisms, their systematic classification remains a mystery. Some appear quite simple and perhaps primitive, while others have fantastic, seemingly highly evolved adaptations to the particular conditions on Pandora.

Most intriguing is the presence of life-forms that have characteristics of both plants and animals. These *zooplantae* (or, colloquially, "planimals") have incipient nervous systems that give them the kind of organic intelligence found in primitive animals. This discovery continues to baffle and delight biologists and botanists who must reassess their preconceptions about the mechanics of life.

As with most everything here, this mystery awaits further study by scientists lucky enough to make it to Pandora.

HELICORADIUM SPIRALE

COMMON NAME: Helicoradian

NA'VI NAME: *Loreyu,* or "beautiful spiral"

TAXONOMY: *Helicoradium spirale.* Root meaning "spiral."

BOTANICAL DESCRIPTION: Tall, herbaceous zooplantae with animal-like nervous system. Single large spiral orange leaf. Responds to touch by coiling up and retracting rapidly into the ground.

HEIGHT: 6 to 8 meters

SPREAD: Leaves can be 2.5 meters wide

ETHNOBOTANY: Leaves used to make ornate ceremonial robes. Orange pigments in leaves extracted and used for paint.

The helicoradian is a type of "sensitive zooplantae" that responds to touch by coiling up so that the single large leaf is no longer exposed to any herbivores that would eat it. Because it grows in clusters, the touch response, or thigmonasty, by one helicordian often triggers the same response in others growing nearby so that the entire population recoils, one plant after another. This retraction is both defensive and an effective feeding mechanism to trap insects and small animals.

Unseen contractile roots belowground aid in the retraction of each folded plant quickly into the ground. The reaction is so swift that it appears that the helicoradians are being sucked into the ground. The Na'vi are able to wander among the helicoradian without triggering this defense response, but are warned of the presence of danger when the helicoradian start to retract.

The large, beautiful leaf of the helicoradian is sometimes collected and used by the Na'vi, although they are careful not to overharvest this unusual life-form and deplete its population. The brilliant orange pigment is extracted and used as paint, and the leaves are used for garments, tents, and sacks.

> Touch response provides defense against being eaten. Plant movement signals presence of danger to Na'vi. Often grows in clusters, where movement of one plant triggers all to retract.

BELLICUM PENNATUM

COMMON NAME: Warbonnet fern

NA'VI NAME: *Eyaye*

TAXONOMY: *Bellicum pennatum.* Root meaning "war" and "feather."

BOTANICAL DESCRIPTION: Large, herbaceous, fernlike plant with colorful iridescent blue leaves. Widely found on Pandora.

HEIGHT: 4.5 to 5.5 meters

SPREAD: 1.5 meters, on average

ECOLOGY: Special pattern of bioluminescence in rays lures insects to plants for nectar. Birds feed on insects and protect plant from insect feeding.

ETHNOBOTANY: Used by Na'vi for ceremonial purposes, including headdresses and other adornment.

The warbonnet fern was aptly named for the primary use of this plant—as headwear during times of both war and peace. The similarity to Native American headwear made from feathers is obvious, as Pandoran colonists have noted.

The most striking feature of the warbonnet fern is the iridescent blue of the leaves, which contain abundant anthocyanin pigments. These pigments are light-reactive chemicals that reflect blue light and that give color to blue and purple flowers and fruit. The warbonnet fern has evolved a close relationship with a particular species of forest bird, which is also a pale iridescent blue color and well camouflaged against the leaves of the plant. These birds feed on insects that are attracted to the blue leaves, which have red lines radiating out from the center of the plant. Insects accumulate on the enlarged central apex or

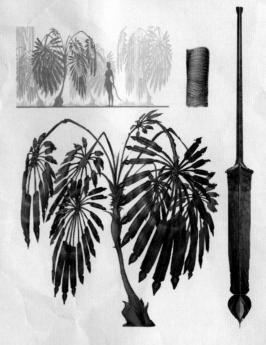

meristem, from which the leaves grow, and the small birds swoop in to feed.

It is fortunate that warbonnet ferns sprout readily from belowground buds because they are gathered and used regularly by the Na'vi. The dark nights are often illuminated by single leaves that have been mounted on trees with their glowing arrowlike pattern pointing to a special destination, reminiscent of Terran neon signs.

> Leaves with bioluminescent lines and arrow-like patterns are used for directional markers and navigation.

COMBATING THE PERVASIVE NET AND OTHER TRACKING TECHNOLOGIES, SYMPATHIZERS ON PANDORA ARE STUDYING TRADITIONAL FORMS OF NAVIGATION AND OTHER MEANS OF NONDIGITAL POSITIONING AND COMMUNICATION.

MAGELLUM DELTOIDS

COMMON NAME: Unidelta tree

NA'VI NAME: *Tsawlapxangrr*, or "tall large root." Or, for short, *tsawlapx.*

TAXONOMY: *Magellum deltoids.* Named for Earth explorer Magellan. Same genus as delta tree.

BOTANICAL DESCRIPTION: Understory forest tree with large triangular leaves, spiny stems, and aboveground prop roots. Similar to closely related delta tree, but leaves are nontoxic. Roots contain toxin that kills and digests animal cells. White bioluminescent glow.

HEIGHT: Largest specimens are 9 meters

ECOLOGY: When unidelta and delta trees grow close together, their roots join belowground. Root toxins pass from unidelta to delta tree roots.

ETHNOBOTANY: Unidelta tree is taller than delta tree, and its wood is straight and dense. Used for construction of canoes and paddles, various musical instruments and performances.

The unidelta tree, closely related to the delta tree, has one important difference. Its leaves are not toxic but its roots are highly toxic. When these two trees are growing close together their roots form connections belowground. Through these connections the root toxin in the unidelta tree can pass to the delta tree, making its roots toxic as well.

These two *Magellum* species have coevolved a mutualistic relationship that benefits them both. The unidelta tree shares its root toxin with the delta tree, which does not need to expend energy making its own, and the delta tree shares nutrients with the unidelta tree. The only clue that a transfer of toxin has occurred is a subtle change in the bioluminescent color of delta tree leaves at night, which the Na'vi have learned to identify. Animals have learned to avoid feeding on roots of both trees, making this mutualism an excellent defense for both plants.

The unidelta tree wood is harvested to make canoes, and the thick waxy leaf cuticle is melted down and used for additional waterproofing. The leaves themselves, which contain no toxic elements, are also used to make bowls, since they are naturally waterproofed. The spines are used by the Na'vi to make tools as well as weapons for hunting and fishing. Because of their close array, the unidelta is the tree of choice for a performance of the pendulum drum.

Log Drums

FUNCTION: Music for social celebrations, rituals

SIZE AND WEIGHT: Various

MATERIALS AND CONSTRUCTION: Fallen logs hollowed out by insect larvae and natural decay, covered on both ends by tanned hide of hexapede. Wood sticks used as beaters.

> Small drums played by individual Na'vi for social dances. Large drums played by four or five Na'vi simultaneously during rituals.

Drums are used as musical accompaniment during all social celebrations and most rituals. Na'vi drums are log drums, usually created out of fallen trees or branches that have been hollowed out by larvae and by the natural decaying processes on Pandora. They are created from a short section of a hollow log. Both ends of the log are covered by the skin of a hexapede.

The best of these log drums are said to be from a fallen unidelta tree. During its life, this tree usually serves as a host for a species of insect with glowing larvae that drill elaborate pathways throughout the wood of the living tree without affecting the tree's ability to grow. Once the tree (or a branch) has fallen, the larvae move to another tree, leaving the fallen log riddled with channels. These channels give the tree an exceptionally resonant quality.

Any combination of sizes of drums may be used to accompany social dances. But the larger drums, those whose wood has been channeled by the larvae, are only used for ritual functions, especially those rituals that form a part of the Uniltaron, or Dream Hunt. These large drums are played by four or five Na'vi warriors at a time, wielding heavy wooden beaters.

PENDULUM DRUM

FUNCTION: Social, to accompany celebratory dances

NA'VI NAME: *T'riti so jahmka*, also *ganti'a hiru'taya*, or "tree that flies"

SIZE AND WEIGHT: 2.5 meters in height, up to 100 kilograms

MATERIALS AND CONSTRUCTION: Large gourd with both ends cut off. Drumheads (one side only) made from sturmbeest bladders. Drums attached by vines at right angles to the sides of hollow unidelta trees.

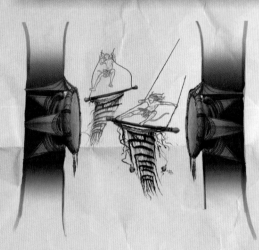

These drums are exceptionally loud, due to the placement of the drums over holes in the trees. When the drum is struck, the volume is amplified by the hollow structure of the tree to which it is attached.

The performer stands on a trapezelike swing; the padded end of the sturdy branch on which he stands acts as the drumstick. He propels himself back and forth between two drums, hitting each as he swings from side to side. Just before the beater hits the drum head, the performer jumps up off the swinging beater, allowing it to rebound naturally. Numerous drums may be played simultaneously by drummers on trapezes of different lengths, creating a chaotic polyrhythm.

Because of the inaccuracy of this swinging/playing technique, a steady rhythm is almost impossible to attain, except by a very few skilled players. Therefore these drums are typically not used as accompaniment for dances. They will, however, be used to ornament songs and especially to add excitement to Dream Hunt dancing.

Injuries are sometimes suffered by clan members who attempt to use the drums during dances at which kava, a mild intoxicant, is consumed.

> Na'vi drummers stand on trapezelike swings, and propel the swings into the drums. Injuries possible, but wildly festive.

PENNANEMONOID CILIARE

COMMON NAME: Anemonid

NA'VI NAME: *Fngapsutxwll*, or "metal-following plant"

TAXONOMY: *Pennanemone ciliare*, or "leafy anemonoid" and "hairy"

BOTANICAL DESCRIPTION: Large forest herb with flattened top that resembles the sea anemonoid and has hairlike leaves. Flat, platelike surface is covered with digestive enzymes for trapping insects.

ECOLOGY: The anemonid is largely carnivorous, trapping insects on its flattened, sticky top surface. It is unique among Pandoran plants in that it absorbs small amounts of unobtanium from the soil.

ETHNOBOTANY: Botanical oddity. No known use on Pandora but is being studied for possible export to Earth for use in cleaning polluted soil.

The anemonid is one of several carnivorous plants on Pandora that obtains most of its nutrition from other organisms rather than making its own through photosynthesis. The large, flattened meristem at the top of the plant is covered with a sticky aromatic substance that attracts insects, which are quickly trapped once they land. Digestive enzymes on the plant's surface then break down the insect bodies to obtain nitrogen and other essential elements.

The anemonid is rather unique in another feature—its roots absorb metals from the soil rather than typical mineral elements needed for plant growth. This gives the plant the ability to move in response to a magnetic field, which was named *magnetonasty* by the first scientists who studied this behavior. The anemonids will turn and lean toward anyone walking by carrying a metal object.

Research is under way on Earth to determine whether anemonids could be used in bioremediation to detoxify soil contaminated with heavy metals, or possibly as a tool for mining. Results so far have been inconclusive.

> If export to Earth is allowed, it is likely to be a favorite in the horticulture trade because of its tracking abilities.

IT'S ALREADY HERE: GREAT SUCCESS IN THE TOXIC FIELDS SURROUNDING PITTSBURGH. TREMENDOUS POTENTIAL FOR USE AROUND THE GLOBE.

FLASKA RECLINATA

COMMON NAME: Baja tickler

NA'VI NAME: *Txumtsä'wll,* or "poison-squirting plant"

TAXONOMY: *Flaska reclinata,* or "reclining flask"

BOTANICAL DESCRIPTION: Large plant with inclined, flask-shaped body held up by aboveground prop roots. Cluster of stiff spiny leaves protect a small opening at the top. Atmospheric toxins are absorbed by the plant and dissolve into liquid that accumulates inside.

HEIGHT: 6 to 7.5 meters

SPREAD: 9 to 12 meters

ECOLOGY: The Baja tickler is a new plant growth form described as resembling a hollow tree. It performs an important function by absorbing, condensing, and purifying atmospheric toxins.

The Baja tickler resembles no plant growth form on Earth and is unique on Pandora. It has been described as something like a large hollow tree that usually grows at an incline. A cluster of large spiny leaves adorn the top, and large roots extend out from the underside of the stem, growing into the soil and helping to anchor and prop up the plant. The surface is rough and green due to a dense covering of small mosslike plants that can withstand high temperatures and harsh conditions.

The Baja tickler is one of the most important plants on Pandora. It is also one of the most dangerous. It plays an important role on the moon by helping to detoxify the atmosphere. Toxic gases (mostly volcanic in origin) are absorbed into the plant body, where they dissolve into a pool of watery liquid that accumulates inside. This primeval "soup" periodically builds up pressure and temperature and is squirted explosively in a toxic plume from the top of the plant. The Na'vi recognize both the value and potential danger of the plant and mainly avoid it.

> Extremely dangerous due to periodic explosive squirting of a toxic plume from the top of the plant.

BANSHEBA TERRESTRE

COMMON NAME: Banshee of Paradise

NA'VI NAME: *Awaiei*

TAXONOMY: *Bansheba terrestre,*
Named for the the wailing banshee of Irish
lore. "Terrestre" means "of the earth."

BOTANICAL DESCRIPTION: Large, exotic-looking herb with curved, tubular plant body, long spines, and large edibleseeds. Wind blowing through tubular body creates eerie wailing sound for which it is named.

HEIGHT: 7 meters

SPREAD: 7 to 8 meters

ECOLOGY: Able to detect warmth from living organisms and rotate toward it. Shoots poison tipped spines as defense.

The banshee of paradise is one of the most dangerous plants on Pandora because it can eject poison-tipped spines in a targeted direction. It has the ability to sense infrared radiation (IR), which is emitted from warm objects such as animals and people, and to rotate its tubular body to point toward the source of the IR. Large spines contain toxins in glands on the tips, which can be deadly in large concentrations. When the source of IR comes close to the plant, the spines eject their poisonous tips in the direction of the threat.

The Na'vi sometimes blow through the tubular plant body to make its signature wailing sound as a warning to intruders to stay away.

Although deadly and toxic, the plant is also a food source for the Na'vi. The large seeds of the banshee are attached on the stem opposite to the direction the plant is pointing, making it easy for the Na'vi to harvest them.

> Highly desirable seeds but difficult to harvest by any creature other than Na'vi.

POSSIBLE USE AS DEFENSIVE PERIMETER AROUND FACILITIES. ALSO, RESEARCH ONGOING BY "CAUSE" SYMPATHIZERS ON ORGANIC IR DETECTION.

HARVESTING FRUIT

FUNCTION: Food source

SIZE AND WEIGHT: Various, but can be up to 60 centimeters in diameter and 5 to 9 kilograms

SOURCE: Various trees and plants

DESCRIPTION: Like much of the flora and fauna on Pandora, fruit and vegetables potentially grow to colossal size. Giant fruit growing on a variety of trees near Hometree provide a valuable source of food for the Na'vi. The fruit is dissected to be eaten immediately, or packaged in large leaves for distribution and/or storage.

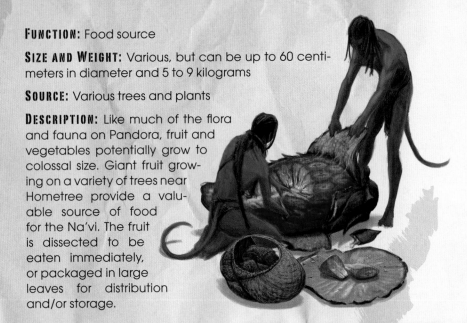

FOOD WRAPS

FUNCTION: Food item, convenient for eating while hunting and gathering but also eaten regularly within Hometree

NA'VI NAME: *Nikt'chey*

SIZE AND WEIGHT: Various, but generally the size of a Na'vi hand

MATERIALS AND CONSTRUCTION: Various food items wrapped in edible leaves and vines from various plants and trees

DESCRIPTION: The Na'vi pride themselves on arranging meats, vegetables, seeds, spices, and fruits into a myriad of combinations. Different Na'vi clans are known for their unique *nikt'chey*, based largely upon local flora and fauna.

BANANA FRUIT

FUNCTION: Food source

NA'VI NAME: *Utu mauti,* or "push fruit"

SIZE AND WEIGHT: 10 to 13 centimeters long, 2.5 to 5 centimeters in diameter

SOURCE: *Utral utu mauti,* or "push fruit tree"

This species grows high in the canopy and, by virtue of its inaccessibility, is considered to be a more special treat. It is considered very lucky to find this species uneaten on the ground, and many Na'vi will wait until they are back at Hometree to show it to others before eating. It is considered good manners to offer the find to a friend or loved one. It is also customary to refuse such an offer while insisting that Eywa meant for the fruit to be enjoyed by the finder. A common joke is to pretend to accept the offered *utu mauti,* and begin to take a bite before then declining and giving it back to the lucky "finder." Everyone laughs at this pretend social transgression, because to accept the gift would be extremely rude. In some young male circles, a would-be recipient pretends to start to eat the fruit, and the finder must wrestle it back in a good natured "fight." On occasion, the fruit is squashed in the process and no one gets it, negating any purported "luck." This is uproarious to Na'vi adolescents.

DESPITE OPPRESSION, THE NA'VI RETAIN A JOYOUSNESS AND DELIGHT IN PANDORA'S BOUNTY. COMMUNITY-ORIENTED, THEY EMPHASIZE PLAY.

LUCINARIA FIBRIATA

COMMON NAME: Binary sunshine

NA'VI NAME: *Penghrrap*, or "danger-teller"

TAXONOMY: *Lucinaria fibriata*, or "fringed lamp"

BOTANICAL DESCRIPTION: Herbaceous plant with bulbous leaves attached close to the main stem. Leaves are strongly bioluminescent. Each leaf can be detached and will grow a new plant from roots at its base. Nervous system gives it animal-like intelligence and response system.

ECOLOGY: Leaves glow with bioluminescence in response to tension and danger. Serve as warning sentinels in the forest.

The binary sunshine is one of many life-forms on Pandora found to have a simple nervous system. These baffling zooplantae continue to be a source of wonder (and some confusion) to scientists. The binary sunshine is also unusual due to its advanced mechanism of bioluminescence. The leaves are modified into enclosed bulbous structures that resemble lamps when they glow. These life-forms are able to detect the presence of danger by sensing the emission of volatile stress hormones from living organisms. For the Na'vi, the colors emitted by the glowing leaves signal whether the landscape is calm or danger is near.

The binary sunshine is adapted for vegetive reproduction in which parts of the organism can reproduce new clonal "planimals" without the need for flowers. When a leaf is removed or falls off a stem it will produce adventitious roots from its base and start growing as an independent planimal. The Na'vi collect the leaves and plant them at crossroads and other key locations to use as sentinels that signal approaching threats.

There is potentially a huge market on Earth for these plants, which could be used as natural landscape lighting that does not contribute to pollution or global warming. The potential effects on Earth's ecosystem are unknown.

Na'vi recognize the level of nearby danger by "reading" the colors of the leaves. Glowing leaves are also used for lighting.

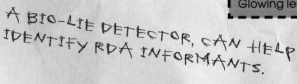
A BIO-LIE DETECTOR, CAN HELP IDENTIFY RDA INFORMANTS.

FELINAFOLIA FERRUGINEA

COMMON NAME: Cat ear

NA'VI NAME: *Pamtseowll,* or "music plant"

TAXONOMY: *Felinafolia ferruginea* Name means "catlike foliage" and "rusty color" ("*ferruginea*").

BOTANICA DESCRIPTION: Woody zooplantae with stem covered in modified leaves resembling cat ears. Wind blowing across the leaves causes a musical sound.

ETHNOBOTANY: The leaves are collected by the Na'vi for use as musical instruments (for *hufwe,* or wind, instruments) and children's toys.

The cat ear plant is an unusual species that is both beautiful and musical, and has the characteristics of both plant and animal. It has cup-shaped leaves, which resemble cat's ears and grow all over the stems. Inside the base of each leaf a small flower forms, giving the appearance of whiskers emerging from the leaf. When wind blows across a stem covered in these specialized leaves, they reflect the waves of sound and form a musical note. Since the leaves vary in size, each tree sounds like a small symphony in the wind.

Besides its musical abilities, this planimal has the uncanny ability to turn in the direction of an animal, and track it as it moves through the rainforest. This can be disconcerting to humans on Pandora, who feel like they are being "watched" as the planimal turns in response to their presence.

It was the behavior of the cat ear that led xenobotanists to discover these odd creatures who straddle the evolutionary fence between plant and animal.

> Birds nest in the many cup-shaped leaves of the cat ear plant.

HUFWE INSTRUMENTS

FUNCTION: Ornamental, musical toys for children

NA'VI NAME: Hufwe, or "wind"

MATERIALS AND CONSTRUCTION: Whizzers made from blade of grass or slender leaf. Flutes are hollow twigs, sometimes with hole cut into twig.

Hufwe instruments require a moving column of air to produce a sound. For example, the whizzer is simply a blade of grass or leaf held loosely between the fingers or the teeth. When blown across, the thin strip of vegetation vibrates rapidly to produce a high-pitched whistle.

The cat ear plant is often used. Leaves of varied sizes can be attached to a base and then tapped with a stick or blown across, which causes air inside to vibrate and generate musical notes. Water added to a leaf reduces the volume of air and changes the note, much like musical bottles played on Earth. An exceptionally skilled player can produce a basic melody, but most of the time the whizzer is used to enliven social dances with brief but frequent whistles.

As soon as they are able, Na'vi children begin to learn the skills they will need to survive as adults. Many of those skills are taught to them using simplified versions of adult social songs. In many cases, games with song, chant, or rhythmic accompaniment teach actual skills like hunting, riding, fire-making, weaving, and food preparation.

Many of the songs deal with the plant and animal life of their world. Through these, children learn the ecology of Pandora: which creatures are friendly and which are not, what things to eat and what to avoid, and the need to show respect for all living things. Other songs, sung by parents and children during quiet family time, teach the mythology and history of the Na'vi as well as the close connection between the Na'vi and their moon.

PSEUDOCENIA ROSEA

COMMON NAME: Chalice plant

NA'VI NAME: *Yomioang,* or "animal eater"

TAXONOMY: *Pseudocenia rosea.* Named for resemblance to Earth's pitcher plant *Sarracenia* and its rosy color. Same genus as direhorse pitcher plant and leaf pitcher.

BOTANICAL DESCRIPTION: Large, beautiful pitcher-shaped carnivorous plant with pale rosy lavender coloring. Contains abundant nectar that attracts small animals.

HEIGHT: Grows 5 to 6 meters above ground

SPREAD: One and a half to two and a half meters at widest point

ECOLOGY: Animals enter the plant, are trapped in the pitcher, and can only move down. Enzymes inside the plant body digest animals for nutrition.

The chalice plant is one of three large pitcher-shaped plants known to exist on Pandora and is the largest carnivorous plant known to man. Its single large leaf is modified into a giant pitcher-shaped tube that is supported by small prop roots at the base. The plant has only a small root system and obtains most of its nutrition from digesting small animals rather than from absorption from the soil. Animals are attracted to nectar and crawl into the tubular plant, where they are unable to exit due to stiff, downward-pointing hairs inside. There they drown in water that collects in the pitcher, and digestive enzymes break down the animal's tissues for absorption by the plant.

> The giant pitchers are large enough to trap a man. Na'vi children learn very early of the danger of chalice plants through songs that are accompanied by a humorous, almost slapsticklike dance.

LOGGED IN THE RDA MORBIDITY AND MORTALITY DATABASE, RESPONSIBLE FOR SEVERAL DEATHS OF COLONISTS.

PSEUDOCYCAS ALTISSIMA

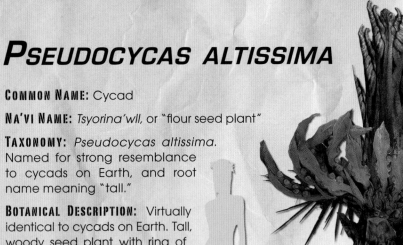

COMMON NAME: Cycad

NA'VI NAME: *Tsyorina'wll,* or "flour seed plant"

TAXONOMY: *Pseudocycas altissima.* Named for strong resemblance to cycads on Earth, and root name meaning "tall."

BOTANICAL DESCRIPTION: Virtually identical to cycads on Earth. Tall, woody seed plant with ring of large leaves at the top. Bears large open conelike structures containing round green seeds.

ECOLOGY: Trunk is covered with symbiotic anemonoid-like organisms that absorb nitrogen and make it available to the plant. Hypothesis (widely dismissed) that it was introduced to Pandora on meteor from Earth.

ETHNOBOTANY: Seeds are soaked to remove nerve toxins and ground up to use as flour

The Pandoran cycad bears an uncanny resemblance to cycads that occur throughout the Earth's tropics. Cycads are ancient seed plants that are found in Earth's fossil record as far back as 208 and possibly even 325 million years ago. They were common during the age of dinosaurs.

Although it is possible that identical life-forms could have evolved on two separate planets, geological and atmospheric differences between Earth and Pandora have led some to speculate that cycads were transported to Pandora from Earth, possibly on a meteor chipped off from the Earth during the Yucatan asteroid strike. Given the remarkable chain of events that would need to have occurred to make this possible, however, most xenobotanists and astronomers dispute this theory.

Cycads on Pandora live in close association with nitrogen-fixing organisms resembling anemonoid that grow on their trunks. They do not accumulate toxins in their tissues the way Earth cycads do, and their seeds can be used as food by the Na'vi and ground up to make flour.

Since cycads have become rare on Earth, botanists are studying the possibility of exporting specimens from Pandora. Though the nitrogen-fixing role would be accomplished by a blue-green algae in the roots, similar to Earth cycads, it is believed that the symbiotic anemonoid would not grow in Earth's atmosphere. These algae produce a neurotoxin that can create symptoms similar to Lou Gehrig's disease. Yet the beauty and rarity of the plant may still make it an attractive item in the horticulture trade.

On Earth, the broad distribution of cycads and the presence of unique specimens on every continent suggest they might have been present even before the breakup of the supercontinent Pangaea.

CHANCES OF EARTH SPORE TRAVELING TO PANDORA ARE INFINITESIMALLY LOW. MORE RDA PROPAGANDA TO VALIDATE THEIR PRESENCE ON THE MOON.

Introducing Pandoran Plants and Animals to Earth

On twenty-first century Earth, invasions of plants, animals, microbes, and other organisms were commonplace due to global trade and travel. Many introductions of exotic species to new lands on Earth were intentional, as they are used for food, feed, fiber, fuel, horticulture, pets, or other purposes. Some, however, were unintentional, and some deliberately introduced species escaped, naturalized, and spread far beyond their points of entry if the new environment was favorable and natural enemies were absent. Although some invasions were seemingly benign, invasive species could profoundly impact native biodiversity and permanently alter natural ecosystems.

Many species slip into new habitats and go virtually undetected for many years as their numbers expand, while others are monitored and regulated carefully from the outset. Known invasive plants and many exotic pests and diseases may end up on government watch lists and legal authority is assigned to federal, state, or local jurisdictions to prevent new introductions and eradicate existing ones.

Such is the case a priori for Pandoran plants and animals if they are ever brought to Earth. Even if they survived, their impact on Earth's environments and biota would be unpredictable until extensive research was conducted. History has shown that even a simple microscopic disease organism introduced to a new susceptible region could wreak havoc on native species as well as humans, so the novelty is probably not worth the risk.

WHO CARES? ACTIVE DISINFORMATION IS STANDARD-ISSUE RDA, A WAY OF CONTROLLING ALL COMMERCIAL ACTIVITY RELATED TO PANDORAN PLANT LIFE. ANYTHING THAT CAN HELP US SAVE OURSELVES IS WORTH THE RISK.

PSEUDOPENTHES CORALIS

COMMON NAME: Dakteron

NA'VI NAME: *Yomhì'ang,* or "small animal (insect) eater"

TAXONOMY: *Pseudopenthes coralis.* Named for resemblance to nepenthes, a carnivorous plant on Earth, and to sea coral.

BOTANICAL DESCRIPTION: Herbaceous vine with elaborate modified leaf for trapping insects. Showy flower has bulbous coral-like structure that emits fragrance to lure insects.

HEIGHT: Roughly 60 centimeters

SPREAD: Roughly 60 centimeters

ECOLOGY: Vine that grows from the ground and ascends to great heights by climbing on trees

The dakteron bears some resemblance to a well-known insectivorous plant on Earth, nepenthes, one of the pitcher plants. Similar to its namesake, the dakteron has a large leaf modified into a hanging pitcher, with stiff, downward-pointing hairs inside that prevent any

captured insects from exiting out the top. Other leaves on the plant are more typical and have an expanded blade, although they are largely blue in color.

The flower of the dakteron is an elaborate structure with two large bulbous appendages arising from the base. The many pores on these appendages give them the appearance of sea coral. These bright blue structures emit a lovely fragrance that is attractive to insects. Lured by the scent, insects land on the leaf pitcher and crawl inside searching for food, only to be trapped and ultimately digested by the plant.

The remarkable effectiveness of the dakteron in trapping insects is put to good use on Pandora. Pieces of the stem are planted near dwellings, where they will take root and grow leaf pitchers that keep the area free of biting insects. This may have applications for equatorial infestation regions on Earth.

> Used and cultivated around dwelling places as a natural insect trap.

EXPERIMENTS BY "CAUSE" ORGANIZERS ONGOING WITH SOME SUCCESS TO DATE ON REDUCTION OF RIVER BLINDNESS ON EARTH AND OTHER INSECT-PROLIFERATED DISEASES OF THE EYE.

CANDEA INFLATA

COMMON NAME: Dandetiger

TAXONOMY: *Candea inflata.* Root name means "sparkle." Also named for inflated stem.

BOTANICAL DESCRIPTION: Large tree with inflated trunk, elaborate bark, and long, slender tubular leaves in a cluster at the crown. Produces abundant resin in the trunk, which accumulates in leaf tips. When resin builds up, leaf tips glow brightly, indicating that resin will be released.

HEIGHT: 12 to 15 meters

SPREAD: Slender trunk of .5 to 1 meter. Crown of tree is 3.5 to 4.6 meters

ECOLOGY: Serves important ecosystem function by absorbing atmospheric toxins, which combine with plant oils to produce resin

ETHNOBOTANY: Resin is collected for use as an adhesive by Na'vi

The dandetiger is a large stately tree that resembles a sparkler. It produces no branches, and all leaves are clustered at the crown of the tree. The leaves are long, slender, tubular, and their flexible structure allows them to sway in even a light breeze. The bark of the dandetiger is elaborate and armored to prevent insects and animals from penetrating it.

The dandetiger accumulates atmospheric gases and combines them with essential oils to produce resin, a complex plant liquid with many uses. In the plant it serves as a defense against damage by insects and disease-causing organisms. The dandetiger transports resin to the leaves, where it accumulates in glandular hairs, or trichomes, at leaf tips. At night the leaf tips glow brightly indicating the presence of the resin.

As resin accumulates it is exuded from the leaf tips from which it rains down on anything below. Solidified resin balls are collected and used by the Na'vi as a natural adhesive due to their mucilaginous texture. Samples of dandetiger resin have been taken to Earth for further study to evaluate its potential as a new plastic and/or a sustainable biofuel.

MORE EFFICIENT FUEL SOURCE THAN ANY KNOWN TERRAN VEGETIVE MATTER. ACCORDING TO OUR RESEARCH, REMARKABLY EFFICIENT IN ITS ENERGY YIELD. INFORMATION AND APPLICATIONS INTENTIONALLY SUPPRESSED BY RDA TO CONTROL GLOBAL MARKET IN ENERGY FUTURES.

ALOEPARILUS SUCCULENTUS

COMMON NAME: Dapophet

NA'VI NAME: *Paywll,* or "water plant"

TAXONOMY: *Aloeparilus succulentus.* Resembles aloe on Earth; name means "aloe-like" and "fleshy."

BOTANICAL DESCRIPTION: Plant with thick trunk and large, succulent spine-tipped leaves at the top. Smaller, saclike, succulent green leaves grow along stem.

HEIGHT: Up to 2.5 meters in height

SPREAD: 1.5 meters

ECOLOGY: Succulent leaves on stem store water and are eaten by thirsty animals. Top leaves eject spines toward stem when too many leaves are removed.

The dapophet is an unusual plant that stores water in its tissues. The leaves to the top of the plant have a gelatinous substance inside that has healing properties when applied to skin. The Na'vi use it to soothe skin that has been burned as well as to speed healing of cuts and other injuries. The leaves can be ground up and ingested to soothe upset stomachs and cure other intestinal ailments.

The fleshy, succulent leaves that grow along the stem are water-filled and very popular with the Na'vi as a portable hydration system. They will pull off the leaves and carry them along to suck on for water. When a leaf is pulled off, a new one grows in its place. The leaves must be harvested carefully, however, because the top leaves occasionally eject spines in the direction of the stem when too many water-filled leaves are removed.

MULTI-USE PLANT IS STAPLE OF NA'VI LIFE. LEAVES AT TOP HAVE MEDICINAL AND HEALING PROPERTIES. NA'VI HARVEST SUCCULENT LEAVES TO CARRY AND EAT FOR HYDRATION. VISCOUS SAP IS ALSO POWERFUL INSECT REPELLANT. DIFFICULT TO OVERSTATE THE PROFIT POTENTIAL FROM PHARMACEUTICAL APPLICATIONS.

CROQUEMBOUCHE COLUMNARE

COMMON NAME: Episoth

NA'VI NAME: *Pxorna'*, or "exploding seed"

HEIGHT: 7.5 to 9 meters

SPREAD: 1.5 to 1.8 meters at base

TAXONOMY: *Croquembouche columnare.* Named for resemblance to dessert of stacked cream puffs, and columnar shape.

BOTANICAL DESCRIPTION: Tall tree with narrow leaves on long branches. Abundant flowers and large spiny fruit produced. Explosive fruit disperse seeds covered in mucilage that stick to anything on contact.

ETHNOBOTANY: Seeds are edible and delicious. Mucilage is collected as skin rejuvenator. Huge potential market in cosmetics and/or industrial solvents.

The episoth is a tree with a highly evolved dispersal mechanism to spread its seeds near and far. The large spiny fruits grow from flowers all along the branches. When they are ripe they open explosively, flinging seeds in all directions. The seeds are covered in q mucilaginous sub-

stance, much like chia on Earth that was used to make a twentieth-century product called "chia pets," although the episoth mucilage is quite acidic. After the sticky seeds adhere to whatever they contact, such as other trees, animals, or Na'vi, the acidic mucilage begins to dissolve the surface layer. This creates a more suitable surface for the seeds to stick and begin germination.

The Na'vi gather the seeds and collect the mucilage to use as a skin rejuvenation treatment. The seeds are delicious and used as a high-protein food source.

SKIN CANCER RATES AT ALL-TIME HIGH DUE TO OZONE IMPACT. DILUTED AND ADAPTED EPISOTH MUCILAGE IS A POWERFUL SKIN REJUVENATION TOOL, PROMOTING NEW SKIN GROWTH IN ACCELERATED CYCLE. MANUFACTURED IN RDA LABS AND TIGHTLY CONTROLLED.

FLASKA ASCENDENS

COMMON NAME: Hookagourd

NA'VI NAME: *Txll'u*

TAXONOMY: *Flaska ascendens.* Root meaning "flask" and "going up."

BOTANICAL DESCRIPTION: Tall, hollow urn-shaped carnivorous plant. Branches on plant body enlarge at the base and eventually break off. Branches form new plants when they root on the ground.

ECOLOGY: Flowers on ends of branches attract birds and small animals. Animals are trapped in the one-way tubular branches and can only move down. Enzymes inside the enlarged plant body digest animals for nutrition.

ETHNOBOTANY: Na'vi harvest the branches to make bowls and jars

The hookagourd is a carnivorous plant that traps and digests birds and small animals to obtain nutrients, which are needed since it has only a small root system. Each branch has a flower at the end with a strong fragrance and abundant nectar that attracts the unsuspecting prey. Once an animal lands on the flower, it crawls deeper into the tubular stem to obtain nectar and is unable to exit due to stiff, downward-pointing hairs. A distinctive feature of the hookagourd is the enlarged base of each branch, which indicates that it is filling up with organic matter from digested animals.

The Na'vi harvest the branches of the hookagourd to carve out bowls and jars for their use. The large basal "gourd" is left intact to grow new branches, thus making the plant a natural factory for production of usable products. Earth botanists on Pandora have discovered that the plants can be manipulated to produce matching sets of bowls if all branches are fed animals simultaneously. These Pandoran rarities are extremely valuable on Earth.

SEVERAL BOWLS MADE FROM PLANT HAVE FOUND THEIR WAY INTO MUSEUMS OR PRIVATE COLLECTIONS OF RDA EXECUTIVES. SO MUCH FOR THE "DANGER" OF EXPORTING PANDORAN PLANTS TO EARTH.

FUNGIMONIUM GIGANTEUM

COMMON NAME: Octoshroom

NA'V NAME: *Torukspxam,* or "great leonopteryx fungus" (so-called due to enormity of both the fungus and its filament system)

TAXONOMY: *Fungimonium giganteum.* Name means "giant fungus."

BOTANICAL DESCRIPTION: Giant purple fungus with umbrella-shaped fruiting body similar to mushrooms on Earth. Bioluminescent with bright purple glow and highly toxic.

HEIGHT: Up to 3 meters

SPREAD: Bell can be 3 meters

ECOLOGY: Has giant underground network of filaments that absorb decayed matter in the soil. Able to live off most of the minerals and toxins on Pandora, including some that are radioactive.

The octoshroom resembles a giant purple mushroom that grows as large as many plants on Pandora. This fungus is presumed to grow large due the low gravity and dense atmosphere of Pandora, although some botanists think its gigantism is due to irradiation by its underground exposure to radioactive uranium oxides and isotopes of xenon.

Most of the body of the octoshroom lives underground in the form of an extensive network of filaments called mycelia. Some of the mycelia penetrate plant roots and absorb carbohydrates while providing the plant with a greater supply of mineral nutrients. The octoshroom is able to absorb and break down nearly everything in the soil, including ammonia, methane, chlorine, various forms of nitrogen, and xenon. Closer study showed that the octoshroom is also a radiotropic fungus that can use ionizing radiation as energy for growth. A similar type of fungus was discovered on Earth after the Chernobyl nuclear accident of 1986, but its metabolism was not fully understood until the giant octoshroom was discovered on Pandora and studied further.

Spores of the octoshroom will germinate and grow new filaments wherever they land. It is possible that the spores of the octoshroom have found their way to Earth via one of the interstellar vehicles, although no specimens have been discovered there yet. Study is under way to determine the efficacy of the mushrooms for pharmaceuticals and bioremediation.

VISUALIZE ACRE UPON ACRE OF THESE PLANTED IN THE NEVADA TOXIC FLATS. COULD HELP RESTORE THE ENTIRE REGION. INCOMPLETE DATA ON ADAPTABILITY TO TERAN ATMOSPHERE.

Tea made from roots of octoshroom is a powerful antivenom effective against the sting of arachnids and other poisonous insects. Too much can be toxic and even lethal.

SALTARUS PENDULUS

COMMON NAME: Beanstalk palm

NA'VI NAME: *Tautral,* or "sky tree"

TAXONOMY: *Saltarus pendulus,* or "weeping dancer"

BOTANICAL DESCRIPTION: Forest tree with tall trunk and long straplike leaves. Can grow to exceptional heights due to low gravity on Pandora. Same genus as razor palm.

HEIGHT: Mature trees can reach more than 150 meters

SPREAD: Up to 15 meters

ECOLOGY: When trees are short they provide abundant shade. Canopy of leaves is used by many birds and animals for nesting.

ETHNOBOTANY: Fibrous leaves are used for making hammocks and baskets. Older trees are used as lookout posts.

The beanstalk palm is named for its ability to grow to exceptional heights in the dense atmosphere and low gravity of Pandora. When it is young, a tree provides shade, and its leaves can be harvested for their fibrous tissue. They are used to weave mats, baskets, banners, and bridles and saddles for direhorses. Unlike its relative the razor palm, the beanstalk palm has rough but not sharp bark and is easy to climb. Birds and small climbing animals are often found nesting in its canopy.

Once a tree matures, it continues to grow to heights not seen on Earth, which places the canopy above most other trees on Pandora. Those not afraid of heights can climb to the top, although on windy days the trunks flex and sway and climbing can be dangerous. The leaves can be used to make a harness to hold the climber onto the tree during the ascent. The Na'vi use the taller trees as lookout posts and launching sites for banshees.

MARACA AERII

COMMON NAME: Panopyra

NA'VI NAME: *Tawtsngal,* or "sky cup"

TAXONOMY: *Panopyra aerii.* Named for resemblance to musical instrument and for growth habit "in the air."

BOTANICAL DESCRIPTION: Succulent, leafless, cup-shaped plant that grows attached to other plants. Considered to be zooplantae because of primitive sensory cells at growing tips of vinelike stems that emerge from the cup. Cells resemble emergent nervous system.

HEIGHT: 15 centimeters at cup

SPREAD: Up to 46 centimeters at cup, but most are roughly 30 centimeters

ECOLOGY: Cup-shaped body catches water and minerals from dew and fog. Tentacle-like vines sense and attract prey. Insects and small animals drown and are digested.

ETHNOBOTANY: Vines used for making nets and traps. Liquid that collects in cup-shaped plant body used for healing properties.

The panopyra is an unusual life-form that has characteristics reminiscent of a jellyfish. It doesn't resemble any taxonomic plant group found on Earth and appears to represent a new line of evolution toward a primitive nervous system. Sensory tissue and a saprophytic lifestyle, where nutrition is obtained from decayed organic matter and dead organisms, place this species somewhere between plants, animals, and fungi. It is an epiphyte and typically grows attached to other plants, sometimes high in the canopy.

Normal plant gravitropic responses are missing in the panopyra. Instead of growing toward or against gravity, the vinelike stems sense and grow toward prey, which in turn are attracted by slight electric signals emanating from the plant stems. Once an animal approaches the panopyra it is further lured by the nutrient-rich water trapped in the cuplike plant body. This double attractant system results in abundant food for the panopyra, which has no need to make its own by photosynthesis.

The Na'vi collect the liquid that catches in the body and use it for a nutritious and healing drink. The flexible stems are used for making nets, traps, and other woven items. The growing tips of the stems with their sensory cells are said to be an attractant and aphrodisiac and are often worn by young Na'vi who are looking for a mate.

Nicknamed "love flower" by Terran scientists.

MARKET FOR STIMULANTS AND "ENHANCERS" REGULATED BY THE RDA. HIGH DEMAND.

CAPSULATUM VIRGATUM

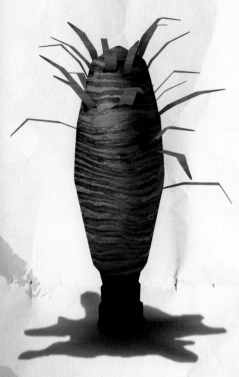

COMMON NAME: Popsicle

NA'VI NAME: *Somtfilor,* or "hot beaty"

TAXONOMY: *Capsulatum virgatum.* Named for capsule shape and "striped" appearance.

BOTANICAL DESCRIPTION: Herbaceous plant with colorful capsule-shaped stem with alternating horizontal stripes of green and pink. Thin, straplike orange leaves protrude in whorls from the stem.

ECOLOGY: Absorbs xenon from the soil and air and stores it in the enlarged stem. Performs important detoxifying function by neutralizing radiation.

The popsicle's chubby shape and bright, colorful surface might lead one to think it belongs on a playground. However, it is neither inert nor harmless. Its bright colors are produced by electrical discharge from the chemical gas xenon, which is found in high concentrations on Pandora. The popsicle plant takes up xenon from the soil and absorbs it from the air and transports it into specialized cells in the stem, where it is stored. These cells possess giant organelles called vacuoles that can sequester high concentrations of xenon, including unstable isotopes that undergo radioactive decay. Popsicle plants are usually several degrees warmer than the surrounding environment due to the reactions occurring in the vacuoles. Storage products remain in vacuoles for the life of the plant and are not excreted.

Research is under way on Earth with the popsicle to determine whether it could be used in bioremediation to decontaminate soil following nuclear testing. On Pandora the plants are generally left alone.

No known use to Na'vi. To be avoided due to low levels of radioactivity and potential to explode.

OBESUS ROTUNDUS

COMMON NAME: Puffball tree

NA'VI NAME: *Rumut,* or "ball tree"

TAXONOMY: *Obesus rotundus.* Root name means "fat" and "round." Same genus as puff daddy and vein pod.

HEIGHT: Larger trees grow well over 15 meters

SPREAD: Widest branches extend 6 meters

BOTANICAL DESCRIPTION: Tall tree with large globular structures produced on ends of branches. Absorbs toxic gases from atmosphere and sodium from soil.

ECOLOGY: Important plant for detoxifying the atmosphere. When globular structures reach maximum capacity they detach and float off into the atmosphere.

ETHNOBOTANY: Na'vi harvest leaves to extract salt for their diets and to feed animals

The puffball tree is considered a keystone species on Pandora. It plays a critically important role in maintaining the stability of the environment. The globular balls produced at the tops of the trees and ends of the branches act as sponges, absorbing toxic chlorine gas from the atmosphere. This function is similar to that of the plant vacuole at the cellular level, which sequesters plant waste products and other molecules such as pigments and minerals.

Although not generally a dangerous tree, Na'vi have learned to be wary of the gas balls, which can explode unexpectedly. The explosion creates a wide dispersal area for the plant's seeds.

The puffball tree also takes up naturally occurring sodium from the soil, much of which is extruded onto the surface of the leaves. The Na'vi collect the leaves to use the salt in their diets. Humans on Pandora discovered this important function of the puffball tree and returned samples to Earth to study its potential use in areas where overfarming and runoff have resulted in salty, unusable soil. Research is ongoing.

> Large balls occasionally explode from buildup of high concentrations of hydrogen gas and sodium hydroxide.

SCORPIOFLORA MAXIMA

COMMON NAME: Scorpion thistle

NA'VI NAME: *Txumpaywll*, or "poison-water plant"

TAXONOMY: *Scorpioflora maxima*. Name means "large scorpion-like plant."

BOTANICAL DESCRIPTION: Large, herbaceous plant with single gigantic colorful flower at its tip

ECOLOGY: Flowers of the scorpion thistle are pollinated by large birds. Flowers exude an acidic liquid that clears the soil below the plant and promotes germination of seeds, a form of "plant parenting."

ETHNOBOTANY: Plant sap is collected by Na'vi and used to make medicines and poison hunting darts that injure but do not kill prey.

The scorpion thistle is a rare plant on Pandora that produces a single gigantic flower at the tip of an enlarged stem. This plant has co-evolved with a particular bird species that is its sole pollinator. Similar to the highly coevolved plant-insect pollinator relationships on Earth, this plant-bird pollinator coevolution has resulted in both species resembling each other. The beak of the bird fits perfectly into the small opening of the flower, where it locates nectar and in doing so transfers pollen.

This plant has a specialized mechanism to prepare the soil for its own seeds to grow. A highly acidic liquid is excreted from the flower and drops onto the ground below the plant. This liquid dissolves any other living organisms in the spot where it lands and also breaks down rocks and other large particles into a nutrient-rich seed bed. When seeds are mature and drop from the flower, they land in this "safe site" and germinate readily under the protection of the parent plant. This highly evolved form of "parenting" has rarely been observed in plants.

SALTCELLAR GRACILIS

COMMON NAME: Razor palm

NA'VI NAME: *Pxiut,* or "sharp tree"

TAXONOMY: *Saltcellar gracilis.* Root name means "graceful dancer." Same genus as beanstalk palm.

BOTANICAL DESCRIPTION: Forest tree with long branches bearing narrow straplike leaves. Bark is covered with sharp razorlike spines.

HEIGHT: Largest trees can grow taller than 12 meters

ETHNOBOTANY: Leaves are used as fiber for weaving mats and baskets, although harvesting them without cutting oneself is extremely difficult. Pliability and a sticky, hairlike underside make them the best choice for a banshee catcher.

The razor palm is one of the most useful plants on Pandora. Its fibrous leaves are woven into mats, baskets, and banners, as well as bridles and saddles for direhorses. However, the tough leaves are extremely sharp along their long edges and can cut skin easily. Because the branches are long and the leaves are narrow, razor palm trees have a very open canopy that blows around easily in the wind, making it dangerous to walk near the trees or harvest their leaves unless the air is very still. Even in still air, sharp spines on the bark must be avoided when collecting leaves.

The leaves of the razor palm are used by the Na'vi to make a special "singing cloth," which is woven with thin spaces at certain intervals to create specific musical sounds. The cloth is used to make banners for ceremonial purposes as well as to quiet fussy Na'vi children.

> The open canopy and narrow leaves of the razor palm allow wind to pass through easily, which results in loud whistling sounds as leaves whip around in the wind.

BANSHEE CATCHER

FUNCTION: A bola used to subdue animals. Can also be used as a tie-down.

NA'VI NAME: *Meresh'ti cau'pla,* or "nothing to see"

SIZE AND WEIGHT: Roughly 2 meters long, 5.5 kilograms

MATERIALS: Made from the leaves of the razor palm tree, a sinuous and durable plant similar to a Terran palm frond, weighted at one end with a stone. The plant's sticky, hairlike underside helps fasten the bola to the animal. Edges of the frond are dulled to avoid cutting.

Mastery of the *meresh'ti cau'pla* is an indispensable skill for all Na'vi youth, who begin training with the device (first as a toy, then more formally) at an early age. A Na'vi will spend years developing the proper technique, first on tree limbs and then on the deerlike hexapede. Without proficient skill, a young hunter will fail during a critical stage of Iknimaya, a profound rite of passage in which a Na'vi captures and bonds with his or her banshee.

During Iknimaya a young Na'vi must approach the *ikran* (banshee) and snap the frond quickly so that it wraps around the creature's snout and eyes. (It is this temporary blinding of the animal that gives the lasso its name, *meresh'ti cau'pla*, which translates roughly into "nothing to see," or "nothing in sight to fear, so don't worry.") With the banshee momentarily disabled, the Na'vi is able to leap onto its back and connect the queues of animal and rider. In that moment, sealed by the subsequent first flight, a lifelong bond is established that allows the Na'vi and banshee to ride through the sky with elegant, seemingly effortless coordination.

It should be noted that an imprecise toss of the *meresh'ti cau'pla* has led to the injury or death of many young Na'vi at the hands of an angered banshee.

Baskets

BASIC USE: Storage and transportation of food and matériel

NA'VI NAME: *Feru m'predu'k*

SIZE AND WEIGHT: Various

MATERIALS AND CONSTRUCTION: Complex weave made from flaxlike leaves (including razor palm), wooden plug, twine, and beads

Most Na'vi woven baskets incorporate a design reminiscent of Terran Chinese finger puzzles. The basket's opening and its wooden plug become tighter and more secure as more pressure is applied; when a basket is hung or carried by the plug, it remains sealed, its contents secure. To open the basket, one simply pushes down on the plug or the base, which in turn slackens the weave and allows the plug to be released. A variety of Na'vi baskets share this common design element.

5 HUMAN TECHNOLOGY ON PANDORA

In the pell-mell rush to exploit the Earth, we have fouled the water, the land, and the sky. Corporations have been forced to look outward for profit—to space, to the moon, to Mars, and, finally, to Pandora. Greed, coupled with the depletion of natural resources, has helped create tremendous advances in technology. Uses for unobtanium are still being discovered, which may be a boon for Earth's economy and technology. But the growing hunger for the superconducting substance also represents a continuing threat to Pandora and to the Na'vi.

Once ensconced on Pandora, the RDA found that much existing Earth technology (including weapons and vehicles considered obsolete), worked well in the harsh Pandoran environment. The AMP Suit, for example, was designed with Earth battles in mind, but is perfectly suited to highly toxic Pandora.

RDA's private security force prefers sturdy, simple weapons that have endured decades of use on Earth. Indeed, most of the current equipment on Pandora is third-generation, Earth-issue weaponry. Instead of the latest iterations of ferro-magnetic weaponry now found on Earth, the RDA relies upon traditional bullet casings with explosive charges.

In the decades since arrival on Pandora, the RDA has created a proficient on-moon robotic manufacturing facility that takes care of all its vehicle, weapons, and ammunition needs. All weapons are built to withstand the rigors of Pandora's electromagnetic fields. The various robo-dozers, earth movers, and Slash-Cutters that have decimated the few remaining patches of Terran rainforest also work well. The powerful CARB Weapon System that proved effective in various insurgencies on Earth has now been unleashed on both the creatures of Pandora and on the Na'vi themselves.

Yet the ongoing travel to Pandora, made possible by the antimatter engines of the ISV fleet, may lead to tremendous benefits for the fragile, dying ecosystems of Earth. Once again, our technology contains within it the paradox of salvation and destruction.

RDA

The largest single nongovernmental organization in the human universe, the Resources Development Administration (RDA), has monopoly rights to all products shipped, derived, or developed from Pandora or any other off-Earth location. These rights were granted to the RDA in perpetuity by the Interplanetary Commerce Administration (ICA), with the stipulation that they abide by a treaty that prohibits weapons of mass destruction and limits military power in space.

With its millions of shareholders, the RDA is the oldest and largest of the quasi-governmental administrative entities (QGAEs). But its origins are far more modest. The entity that would become the RDA was little more than a Silicon Valley garage start-up in the early twenty-first century, when its two founders borrowed money from family members to begin the company.

Within a few decades, the company had the stature to propose the construction of a world-spanning rapid transit system that would allow entire population groups to conveniently commute hundreds or even thousands of kilometers to perform work where it was needed, without impinging on the cultural values of host populations. This led to the current global network of maglev trains that require the superconductor unobtanium for their continued operation.

The company's early expeditions to Pandora were seen as a colossal risk; the construction of the ISV *Venture Star* alone put an enormous strain on capital resources. But with exclusive mining rights to unobtanium (which at time of publication is valued at 40 million dollars per kilo), and potential profits from countervirals, biofuels, and cosmetics, the enormous capital investment has paid off.

AVATARS

COMMON NAME: Avatar

NA'VI NAME: *Uniltirantokx, or* " dreamwalker body"

DESCRIPTION: A cloned Na'vi humanoid, initially created in vitro on Earth, and then allowed to grow to maturity during the nearly six-year trip to Pandora. Genetic material from the future human "driver" is incorporated into the avatar embryo, allowing the development of the anatomic structures needed to allow a mental link to be established with that particular individual.

The avatar project was originally intended to create mine workers who did not need environmental protection systems and could eat Pandoran foodstuffs, but the cost of the mental-link system remained too high for the numbers needed. Avatars are now used only for field work and, when the opportunity arises, to interact with the Na'vi and study them. It was hoped that the avatars could act as unofficial ambassadors, but Na'vi have for the most part viewed these hybrid creatures with a mix of contempt and mistrust.

The cloned avatar has the body structure and physiology of a Pandoran native; however, adding to the avatar's DNA the human genes necessary to create the mental-linking ability altered the anatomy to the extent of producing five digits on the hands and feet, and reducing the size of the eyeballs. The reason for this is not known.

ISV VENTURE STAR

FUNCTION: Interstellar vehicle designed to transport personnel, supplies, refined ore, equipment, and data between Earth and Pandora

OFFICIAL NAME: Capital Star Class Interstellar Vehicle *Venture Star*, Hull Number 1

MANUFACTURER: Consortium of aerospace contractors under control of RDA

POWER SOURCE: Hybrid fusion/matter-antimatter

SIZE: Overall length: 1,646 meters. Overall width: 330 meters. Overall height: 218.5 meters.

CRUSING SPEED: 130,200 miles per second or 70 percent of lightspeed. Beamed energy for outbound acceleration phase, hybrid matter-antimatter energy for outbound deceleration phase. Inverse for return to Earth.

The ISV *Venture Star* is one of the ten vehicles designed to travel between Earth and Pandora at maximum acceleration and deceleration to quickly reach (and retreat from) near lightspeed. She was designed

to carry a large payload of supplies and passengers to establish commercial and scientific outposts on alien worlds.

The ship's ultimate mission is the exploitation of indigenous resources on Pandora.

The ship's structure (which, if not for zero gravity, would appear almost flimsy), begins with two side-by-side engines. These are attached to a tether leading to the payload section, which includes habitation for crew and passengers in cryosleep, and the cargo section.

When the first voyage to the Alpha Centauri system was envisioned, engineers realized quickly that a conventional rocket was hopelessly inadequate. Since the starship would have to travel near lightspeed, its rocket exhaust velocity, too, had to be near lightspeed to create sufficient thrust. This eliminated chemically powered rocket engines.

Talk of "dilithium crystals" and "warp drive" captured the imagination of twentieth-century sci-fi fans, but no such inventions have come to fruition. For now, engineers must rely upon techniques that exploit our current understanding of physics. Visionaries set their sights on the potential for matter-antimatter reactions. The enormous energy released in the fusion of matter with antimatter is the only known means of creating the kind of propulsion needed for interstellar travel.

ENGINES

A matter-antimatter reaction causes the annihilation of matter into energy. The antimatter is contained by a magnetic field in a near-perfect vacuum in which it circulates as a high-density cloud of atoms cooled to near-absolute-zero temperature. When antimatter and matter are brought together, they mutually annihilate and produce an enormous amount of energy, which must be directed by a powerful magnetic field to form the exhaust plume. These photons of energy, although massless, possess momentum, and their ejection provides the thrust to accelerate the ship. Additional thrust is obtained by injecting hydrogen atoms into the plasma before it leaves the engines. The exhaust flare is incandescent plasma a million times brighter than a welding arc, and more than thirty kilometers long. The plume is considered to be the most spectacular man-made sights in history.

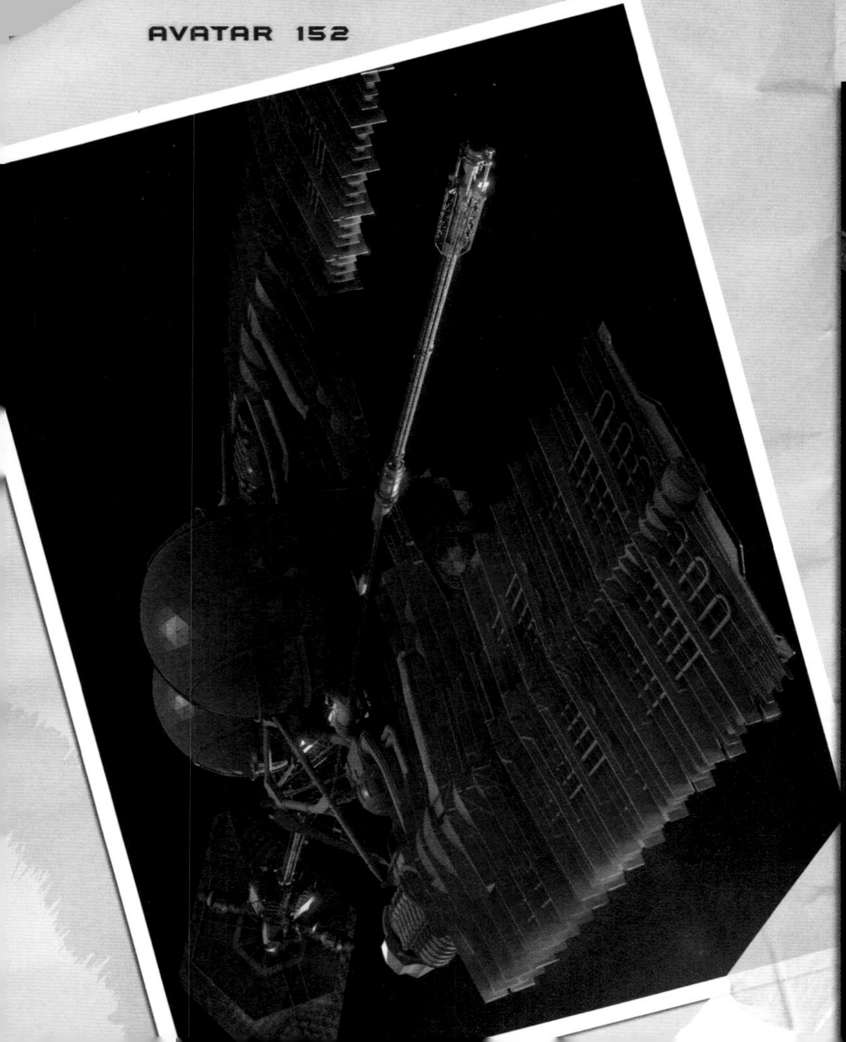

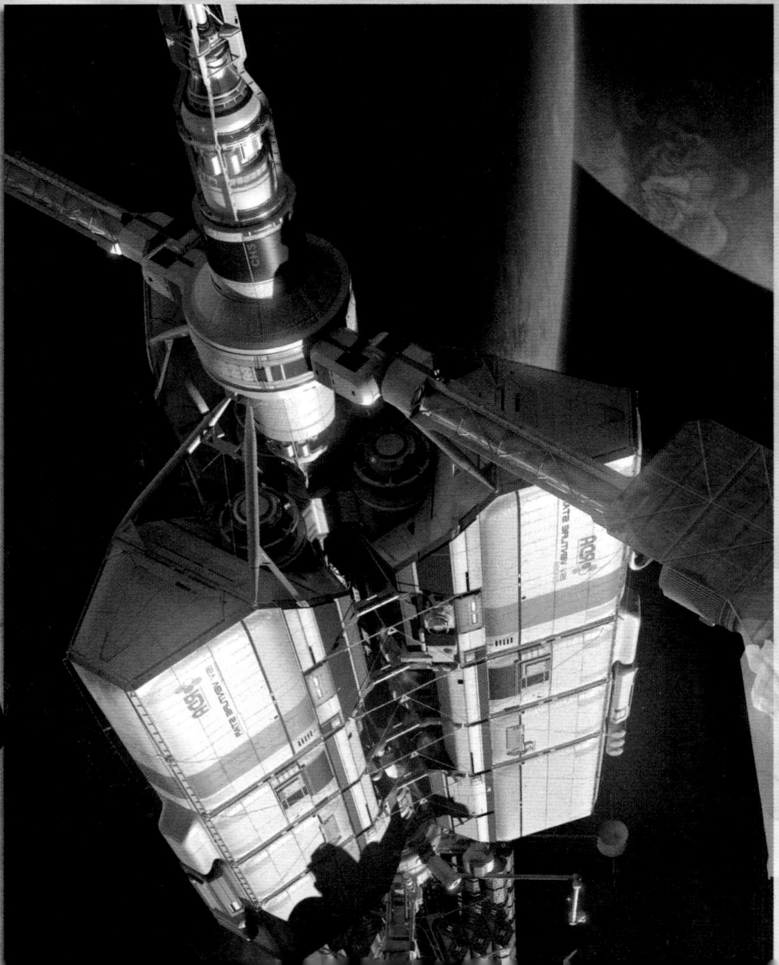

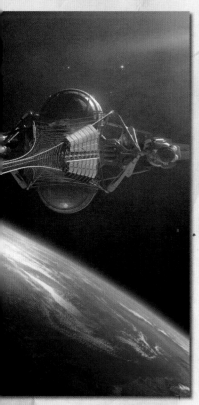

One of mankind's great technological achievements and the embodiment of centuries of theoretical and practical science. Will this vehicle built by greed be our salvation? Perhaps. It took us to Pandora, our beacon, our hope.

CREW AND PASSENGERS

A more detailed look at the payload section reveals the crew habitation modules, which consists of two compartments on the opposite ends of a transverse truss. A pressurized tunnel runs through the truss, connecting the two units.

The general habitation section is an open-truss central core around which the pressurized modules are aligned radially. The core truss contains a pressurized rigid central corridor, with branching connections to each module. Inside each module is an open frame structure of advanced composites, with non-load-bearing walls made of foam composite. There is almost no metal used in the structure. There are a number of airlocks for the crew and repair bots, which look like high-tech mechanical crabs.

The ship's cryobank is housed in this section. Here, dozens of passengers doze peacefully in cryosleep, with bodies kept safe and nourished in chilled cryovaults. Among those put into cryosleep are replacement security forces, miners, scientists, and avatar operators.

Nearby are the amnio tanks used to grow the genetically engineered Na'vi bodies that will be "driven" by their human operators.

MATTER-ANTIMATTER REACTION

FUNCTION: Energy source to power cities on Earth and interstellar spaceships

BASIC PRINCIPLE: When matter and antimatter come into contact, they annihilate each other and produce a tremendous amount of energy.

"Matter" is the general term for any physical substance whose atoms are composed of protons, neutrons, and electrons. Everything on Earth and everything we have found on other planets consists of normal matter.

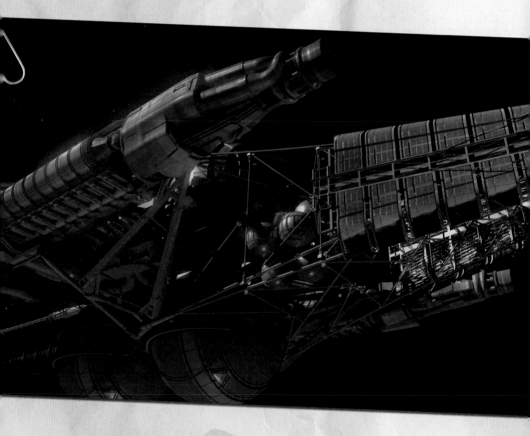

Antimatter is a kind of mirror-image version of normal matter. Its atoms are composed of antiprotons, antineutrons, and antielectrons. It does not occur naturally (except as a minor output of supernovas and black holes), and must be created with high-energy particle accelerators or other devices.

When matter and antimatter combine, they transform into energy in accordance with Einstein's famous equation: $E = mc^2$, where m is the total mass of the matter and antimatter, and c is the speed of light. When c is squared, it is so huge that even a small mass produces a tremendous amount of energy. Just twenty-eight grams of mass totally converted into energy can lift almost two trillion tons thirty centimeters off the ground.

The development of matter-antimatter power reactors was initially seen as the solution to Earth's energy shortage and pollution problems. But the abundant, cheap energy they produced only encouraged the construction of new factories. This in turn created even more drain on Earth's dwindling resources.

In the late twentieth century, Alger Witzhur and Kada n'Goma built the first prototype matter-antimatter power generator. Despite this remarkable breakthrough, the two scientists doubted that their generator would ever be practical for anything less than a major city; it required a massive refrigeration system to maintain the low-temperature superconducting magnets that contained the matter-antimatter reaction! Indeed, a full two-thirds of the first interstellar vehicle was devoted to its power-generating and cooling systems.

But the subsequent discovery of unobtanium, which remains superconducting at very high temperatures, meant that the matter-antimatter reactor no longer required massive refrigeration units. This increased the speed, cargo capacity, and efficacy of interstellar vehicles, which in turn has made the colonization of Pandora a practical reality.

> Enormously powerful, but difficult to contain until the discovery of unobtanium allowed the production of extremely intense magnetic fields without huge energy-consuming refrigeration systems.

SUPERLUMINAL COMMUNICATIONS

FUNCTION: Interstellar communication, currently in use between Earth and the RDA facilities on Pandora

DESCRIPTION: An instantaneous communication system made possible by a loophole in the laws of physics

Until recently, it was believed that information could not be transmitted faster than the speed of light because it must be either in some material form (e.g., a datacube) or modulated on some kind of energy (e.g., a series of short and long laser pulses). To prove otherwise would go against Einstein's hallowed Theory of Relativity.

When physicists began to study individual subatomic particles (protons, neutrons, electrons, photons, muons, neutrinos, etc.) back in the early twentieth century, they found that these miniscule entities did not act according to the laws of classical Newtonian physics.

A new branch of physics, quantum mechanics, was developed to explain the bizarre behavior of subatomic particles. One of the emergent theories postulated that if two "entangled" particles are created, a measurement made on one of them will affect the will affect the measurement of another particle instantaneously, regardless of the distance separating them.

It was not possible to send information using this theory, however, because there was no way to control the state the first particle would have when it was measured. As a result of this random element, there was no way to encode any information in the state of the second particle when it was measured. This phenomenon was tested by multiple experiments, and almost always gave confirmatory results.

Scientists have found many phenomena that seemed impossible at first (some types of radioactive decay, electrical current flowing through insulating materials, etc.) But it was later discovered that subatomic particles can sometimes pass through a barrier (either physical or an energy level) that is theoretically impossible. The "tunneling" mechanism by which this occurs is still unknown, but it appears to be statistically predictable, even when random in nature.

In recent decades, physicist Austin McKinney, a researcher at the Broadlawn Institute, discovered that by imposing an intense oscillating magnetic field on the first entangled particle, a tunneling effect occurred, and he could influence the state it would take when he measured it. This, in turn, instantly controlled the state of the other particle when it was measured, no matter how far away the particle happened to be.

However, the tunneling process was far from perfect. The particle would adopt the desired state only once in ten thousand attempts. The other 9,999 were random. But McKinney was undeterred. He developed a highly redundant, error-correcting encoding scheme and was able to achieve a data transmission rate of three bits per hour. All current Superluminal Communicationss devices are based on his invention.

WE HAVE OUR OWN TRANSMITTER AND RECEIVER.

VALKYRIE SHUTTLE

FUNCTION: Cargo and personnel transport between orbiting interstellar vehicle and surface of Pandora

OFFICIAL NAME: SSTO-TAV-37 B-class Shuttle Craft

NA'VI NAME: *Shah-tell*

SIZE: 80.03 meters wide 101.73 meters long

PAYLOAD: Up to 60 armed troops, 25 AMP Suits, 25 tons of refined unobtanium and/or supplies

RANGE: 2,000 kilometers in atmosphere

SPEED: More than 35,000 knots when leaving Pandora's gravitational field

The Valkyrie is a single stage-to-orbit (SSTO) transatmospheric vehicle (TAV) with a massive payload capacity. The Valkyrie is roughly four times the size of the twentieth-century Earth shuttles. The Valkyrie and other shuttles in use on Pandora have been hardened to resist pervasive magnetic fields. Its cargo bay can hold troops, AMP Suits, all necessary ammo and gear, plus larger payloads, such as specialized lab equipment that cannot be manufactured on Pandora. The inside

of the bay looks much like any Terran cargo airplane, with netting to secure payloads to the walls, rollers built into the floor to facilitate unloading, lock bars for the AMP Suits, and seats for RDA security forces.

But its most important mission is the transportation of refined unobtanium from the surface of Pandora back to an orbiting insertellar vehicle. Without this capability, there would be little or no human presence on Pandora. It is also the only possible ride back to the mothership, and thus the one link with the long highway back to Earth.

When the Valkyrie descends through the sky like an arrow, the atmosphere creates friction that heats the tile-protected nose and leading edges of the delta-shaped wings. It goes into hover mode as it nears the landing pad, looking like a windowless metal skyscraper on its side as it slowly lowers itself to the ground.

The Valkyrie rides on a plume from its dual-mode fusion engine so powerful it can rocket from Hell's Gate to the mothership in less than twenty minutes; it can reach escape velocity without the necessity of achieving multiple orbits to gain momentum.

Despite its size, the Valkyrie's mass is small due to a fuselage fashioned from extremely strong nonmetallic composite material. The material has high tensile strength, but only one quarter of the weight of the permalloys used in previous shuttles. The superstructure uses carbon fiber composite in key locations to maximize stability and help conserve fuel.

The two exhaust ports are located in the rear, and the engine nacelles are heavily shielded from the cargo bay. The least radioactive sections of the reactor directly parallel the bay.

There is a rear hatch that lowers for the unloading of large vehicles and AMP Suits. There are fold-down stools with passive restraints for the individual passengers who line both long walls of the bay. The AMP Suit racks are located in the middle of the cargo bay in a double row.

GROUND ASSAULT VEHICLE

FUNCTION: Assault vehicle designed to travel quickly over uneven land-scape for combat operations

OFFICIAL NAME: GAV (Ground Assault Vehicle) JL-723

SIZE: 3.6 meters long by 1.2 meters wide

RANGE: 1,050 kilometer

NOTES: Soldiers call it "Hellrider," because the gunner must rely solely on body armor to keep him safe.

The GAV Swan is the RDA's all-terrain ground assault vehicle designed to travel across uneven landscape at high speeds. It is heavily armored with permalloy and bristles with weaponry. This brawny, bruising com-bat vehicle is far from pretty; at times looking like a metal giraffe. It is just as effective on Pandora as it has been in Earth's few remaining jungles.

The previous model was called the "Dove," which in the field was considered far too precious an irony. It is now called the "Swan" because of the extended gunner's chair that can rise on a crane up to 3.6 meters above the vehicle to see over obstructions between the gun and the target, like the long neck of a swan. Unfortunately, a hunter can more easily clip a head held high than one held low. So the gunner must ride high and in the open, a primary target for the enemy, even one armed only with a bow and arrow.

The Swan's unstated mission on Earth is to draw fire, suppress fire, or provide a moving target that is less expensive to replace than an AMP Suit or Scorpion gunship.

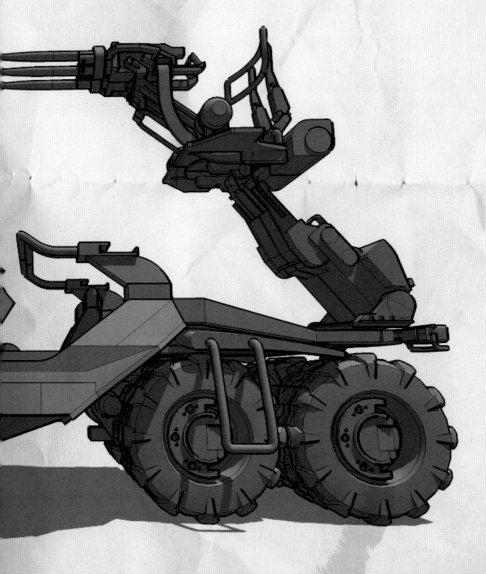

C-21 DRAGON GUNSHIP

FUNCTION: Stable, heavily defended, lightly armored weapons platform and troop transport for combat missions with massive array of weaponry for battle domination

OFFICIAL NAME: C-21 Dragon Assault Ship

NA'VI NAME: *Kunsip apxa,* or "large gunship"

WEAPONRY: Track-and-tack weapons and personnel detection with IFF (Identification Friend or Foe) codes installed and upgraded before every mission. Eight 50-millimeter sentry guns, full array of rocket and missile launchers.

SIZE: 41.15 meters long, 31.7 meters wide

SPEED: 120 knots, fully loaded

RANGE: 2,000 kilometers, fully loaded with up to 30 armed troops and supplies

The Dragon is a lightly armored, four-rotor, turbo-powered assault ship with maximum payload and firepower. It supports four 50-millimeter sentry guns over/under the nose, with two at the tail and one on each side. The forward and aft wing nubs feature an array of rocket and missile launchers. The cockpit is sealed, but the cargo bay opens to the atmosphere.

The unit is as large as the biggest twentieth-century helicopter cargo carriers (the "eggbeaters" of yore), and over twice the length of the Sikorsky Black Hawk. It was designed to lay down devastating suppressing fire that swiftly eliminates enemy positions and armament. Large and slow, it requires armor and multiple guns that overlap each other's range of firing for a complete umbrella of protection against enemy aerial attack (much like the celebrated "Flying Fortresses" of Earth's World War II). The vehicle is considered impenetrable to Na'vi weaponry and Pandoran creatures.

The Dragon can carry thirty armed combat forces, complete with supplies and ammo, or a massive payload of explosives. It can also carry up to ten AMP Suits.

The Dragon was originally developed to defeat aerial or ground troops in the shortest time, using maximum firepower short of a nuclear strike. During wars and rebellions on Earth, the Dragon has earned its reputation as a flying machine easily capable of 100 percent casualties.

Some Dragons have been outfitted with the latest spy technology and can pinpoint targets and bank data for future missions. But the most effective use of this aircraft is to fly directly into enemy positions using all available weaponry for maximum kill.

ENOUGH NONNUCLEAR FIREPOWER TO DEVASTATE AN AREA THE SIZE OF MANHATTAN IN SIX SECONDS. DESPITE ARMOR AND MULTIPLE DEFENSE GUNS, THE DRAGON IS SUSCEPTIBLE TO ENEMY MISSILE STRIKE.

AT-99 Scorpion Gunship

FUNCTION: Escort vehicle for shuttle landing and take-off. Close air support for military sorties from Hell's Gate. Air support for clear cutting and mining operations.

OFFICIAL NAME: AT-99 Gunship

FIELD NAME: Scorpion

NA'VI NAME: *Kunsip*

SIZE: Fuselage is 12.2 meters long, 8.73 meters wide

SPEED: Maximum of 200 knots

RANGE: 1,200 kilometers, fully loaded with passengers and weaponry

NAVIGATION AND COMMUNICATIONS: Forward, side, and down radar and sonar generators

WEAPONRY: Large array of side- and forward-mounted air-to-air and air-to-ground missiles. Two forward-mounted .50 caliber automatic machine guns.

The Scorpion is a highly maneuverable, aerial Mosquito-class targeting and missile launch platform. Difficult for the enemy to track, it utilizes instantaneous targeting with 98.4 percent accuracy to eliminate any threat from the ground or sky. It has proven a reliable and effective countermeasure to urban or jungle insurgencies in which accuracy, speed, and maneuverability are crucial to the success of the mission.

The AT-99 Scorpion Gunship is a twin-turbine, vertical-takeoff-and-landing rotorcraft with half-inch armor plating. Arms are controlled by a standard onboard autofire targeting computer. The cockpit is sealed from outside atmosphere but pressurized with air breathable by humans. The machine looks a little like, and operates better than, a standard twentieth-century helicopter gunship, such as those used in the Vietnam and Iraq Wars.

As a vital strategic link on the RDA's security assault forces, the Scorpion "whiptails" the aerial enemy or ground forces with impeccable targeting accuracy and speed.

The Scorpion was designed to fly in a variety of atmospheres within 15 percent, plus or minus, of Earth's air density. Its twin vertical-lift tilt-rotors operate much like a standard helicopter. But the rotation speed and range of angle are greater, making it an extremely fast and maneuverable machine. Depending on the atmospheric conditions, the top speed of the Scorpion can surpass 200 knots. It can accelerate and decelerate in flight at 2.7 Gs. Maximum rate of climb is 545 meters per minute.

> Distinctive whine of rotors has been known to cause stampedes of Pandoran fauna.

IF THEY'RE COMING FOR YOU, THEY'LL BE FLYING ONE OF THESE. BEST DEFENSE: GET UNDERGROUND.

SA-2 Samson Tiltrotor

FUNCTION: Military and civilian transport for cargo and personnel. Often used for transport of scientists and avatars for missions to remote locations such as the Hallelujah Mountains.

OFFICIAL NAME: SA-2 Samson Tiltrotor

FIELD NAME: Samson

SPEED: Maximum of 144 knots

RANGE: 1,500 kilometers

SIZE: 15.9 meters long, 14.99 meters wide

The Samson Tiltrotor is the RDA's aerial truck designed to carry out mostly noncombat missions. It is often used to drop supplies and personnel at distant field sites. Its heavy-duty crane can carry portable labs for use in the Pandoran rainforest or mountains. The unit features minimal armament for defensive purposes only, making it an easy target in a battle, but the workhorse for the Pandoran project. Its closed-rotor system and cutters on leading edges allow for safe operation in the rainforest.

A launch array below the nose can fire either air-to-air or air-to-ground rockets. Because the weight load is dedicated mostly to cargo and personnel, there is little ammunition on board. As big as a twentieth-century Black Hawk helicopter, the Samson is a midclass, twin-turbo vertical-takeoff-and-landing (VTOL) aerial vehicle with half-inch armor plating. It has been used on Earth for more than one hundred years, but it has been hardened for use in Pandora's electromagnetic fields. Its only onboard armaments are two nose-mounted rocket launchers controlled by a standard autofire targeting computer, and a detachable door gunner station capable of firing out either side of the cargo bay and featuring a detachable 50-millimeter rotary machine gun that fires high-impact, armor-piercing shells.

The cockpit is sealed from the outside atmosphere and pressurized with air breathable by humans. The cargo bay is not pressurized and, on Pandora, humans riding in the cargo bay (which carries up to twelve passengers) must wear their breathing devices to survive.

SAMSONS ARE UNDER CIVILIAN COMMAND. VULNERABLE TO PIRACY.

RDA BOAT

FUNCTION: Military operations and civilian transport

OFFICIAL NAME: 67-1A Liquid Environment Transport

MANUFACTURER: RDA

SIZE: 2.79 meters long, .96 meters wide

SPEED: 45 knots over Earth-ocean density

WEAPONRY: Twin 30-millimeter sentry guns, helmet-mounted "look and lock" target system or manual trigger

The RDA boat is designed to transport goods and personnel over a liquid environment. This includes H_2O, as well as off-Earth liquids of greater or lesser viscosity. The model 67-1A is a four-man craft that provides armed escort for larger transports. The boat can also convey small teams of field operators, avatars, or scientists to sites on islands or banks.

There are seats for two pilots, each with plug-in capabilities to operate the targeting/firing system for the twin 30-millimeter sentry guns that provide the primary defense.

The 67-1A can also function as a stealth rescue boat, which makes it ideal for night missions. With its patented "hush mode" engine, anti-tracking systems, and low physical profile, it can penetrate hostile territory without detection by audio or visual sensors, or by radar or sonar soundings.

The rudderless boat utilizes the latest airfoil technology on either side of its rear-mounted engine to steer the craft across a fluid surface. In addition, it features twin exhaust ports mounted at the edges of the stern plate. By varying the pressure of the fluid expelled out the individual exhaust ports, the boat can be steered. Without the necessity of a rudder, the boat has a much shallower draft that allows it to traverse swamplike environs where there is thick undergrowth and little fluid depth.

SLASH-CUTTER

FUNCTION: Brush clearance for mining operations

OFFICIAL NAME: Slash-Cutter, heavy duty model 10

FIELD NAMES: "Slice-and-dicer," "pizza cutter"

SIZE: Circular blade is 2.74 meters in diameter.

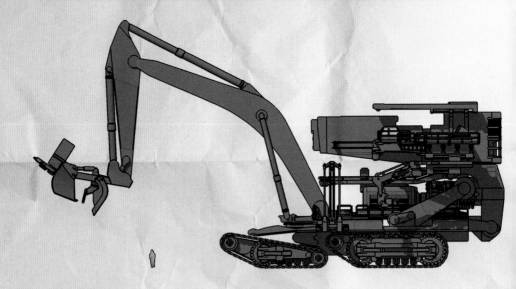

The Slash-Cutter is a razor-sharp rotating disc with angled and beveled teeth made from diamond-hard carbon fiber composite that provides maximum cutting action with minimal wear. The supercooled blade disc will slice through material approaching the density of stone. A large forest of the hardest pine can be felled by just one disc operating continuously for only a few weeks.

There are many ways to clear-cut a forest. You can use explosives to blast them down. You can pull them up by the roots with powerful ripper machines. The Slash-Cutter is the most efficient and effective. The unit is self-sharpening and rarely needs replacing. There are exchangeable heads for the cutter to suit the various densities of materials to be slashed.

The unit is usually installed on a tractor/digger combination unit. The blade functions under extreme stress conditions, slicing through trees equivalent in diameter to the ancient redwoods of the Pacific Northwest at a rate of one per minute. The cutter can be lowered via the crane arm to just above the surface of the ground, leaving only enough stump for the ripper machines to hook onto for extraction.

The computer-designed teeth are angled and beveled for maximum tear ratios, and the debris is rapidly spewed out by the angle of rotation. Operating at tremendous speed between frictionable surfaces, the cutter disc could superheat and melt the rotating shaft and attendant holding gear. But the blade is cooled by a liquid helium spray running down the crane arm and into the Slash-Cutter unit, keeping it within operational temperature limits. The spray requires that all human operators stay clear, which they must do already because of the high-velocity spray of debris.

Nicknamed "pizza cutter" because of resemblance to circular device used for slicing pizza. Proved invaluable in Brazil.

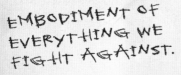

EMBODIMENT OF EVERYTHING WE FIGHT AGAINST.

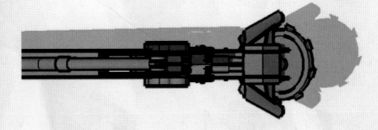

MBS-22A Automated Sentry Gun

Use on Pandora: Perimeter defense

Manufacturer: Masa-Cirre Ltd., Modular Belt Systems Division

Weapon Type: Sentry and mounted patrol

Action: Supersonic projectile

Ammunition: 20-millimeter ball bearings or needles, tracer rounds

Rate of Fire: One barrel: 2,000 rounds per minute. Three barrels: 6,000 rounds per minute.

Selective Fire (via remote control): Sequential, single pulse, or single barrel

Length: 1889.76 millimeters

Height: 1310.61 millimeters

Weight: 110 kilograms

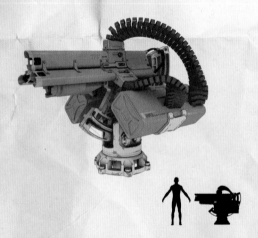

The MBS-22A's primary function on Pandora has been as an automated perimeter defense sentry gun. Situated on towers around Hell's Gate, this weapon can defend against both air and ground attacks at up to 488 meters. It has proven remarkably effective against predatory creatures (both ground and air) that stray too close to the compound.

This particular weapon uses a tri-rail system, which means that it incorporates three barrels that alternate use. This allows the previous rail to cool and reset.

The MBS-22A is an auto-targeting weapon system, developed and manufactured initially by Masa-Cirre, a Portuguese-French arms conglomerate. The weapons system technology was later licensed for manufacture by other armament companies under the name "Masa-Cirre Ltd." Although it has various hardware manufacturers, it is still commonly referred to by its original name because the software implementation is retained by the parent company. The software, known as MBS (Modular Belt System), is widely used on various weapons platforms, such as aircraft, armored personnel carriers, fixed defensive positions, etc.

> Weapon has a unique muzzle flash that displays a sequential triangle pattern.

Bush Boss FD-11

USE ON PANDORA: Flamethrower for use with AMP Suit. Industrial defoliant, but can be used against fauna as well.

MANUFACTURER: Bush Boss portable chemflame defoliant devices

WEAPON TYPE: Chemical-thermal incinerator

LENGTH: 1828.80 millimeters

WEIGHT: 90.7 kilograms dry

By having this weapon system hand-operated by the AMP Suit driver (as opposed to a fixed-point weapon system), the mission configuration is customizable based upon the needs of the specific operation. This device is a defoliant, used primarily to clear an area of leaves and smaller plants prior to the use of earth movers. Its primary use to date has been during AMP Suit perimeter patrols around Hell's Gate. Bush Boss makes a wide range of useful tools for terrain alteration and control. The FD-11 is a custom design for exclusive use with the AMP Suit. Its smaller system, the FD-3, can be used without the AMP Suit.

GAU 90 30-MILLIMETER CANNON

USE ON PANDORA: For use with AMP Suit. Clearing of dense underbrush and vines inhibiting the movement of driver.

MANUFACTURER: Hirte and Fahl Arms Manufacturing Ltd.

TYPE: Automatic cannon, gas-cooled

AMMUNITION: 30-millimeter HEI (high explosive, incendiary), penetration and tracer rounds

LENGTH: 2194.6 millimeters

WEIGHT: 100.7 kilograms

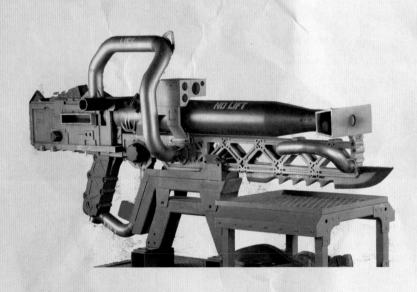

The Gau 90 can be used as a conventional weapon against larger creatures and indigenous tribes. But it is most often used as an effective clear-cutter. The high explosives provided by this cannon have proved useful in the rapid clearing of paths through the dense foliage of Pandora. This Gau 90 is also fitted with an H&F Arms Manufacturing Ltd. FPCT (fixed-point cutting tool). This modular attachment allows the AMP Suit drivers to use the Gau 90 underside as a brush and wire clearing tool when operating in dense foliage or urban environments. The form factor of the underside cutting tool (looking like a large traditional "bayonet") is a design choice borrowed from its sister module, the AMP-H&FAML-SK, which proved very popular with buyers and operators associated with the AMP Suit weapons system.

AMP Suit Knife

Use on Pandora: Clearing dense underbrush and vines inhibiting movement of the AMP Suit

Manufacturer: Hirte and Fahl Arms Manufacturing Ltd.

Length: 1066 millimeters

Weight: 34 kilograms

The form of this device, which looks like a large knife, was a deliberate design choice by the manufacturer; early prototypes with this admittedly comic shape proved very popular with defense buyers and AMP Suit drivers. As a consequence, the more practical "square" and "V" cutters were eventually phased out in favor of the large knife shape. Originally fixed to the underside of the AMP Suit forearm, this was later changed to modular "free" use. This proved safer during nonlethal riot control, when the AMP Suit used by police did not include a large, fixed cutting edge. On Pandora, the ceramic blade is used primarily as a path-clearing tool when the AMP Suit vehicle is moving through dense brush environments.

Wasp Revolver

USE ON PANDORA: Protection against large animals, indigenous population

MANUFACTURER: Masa-Cirre

NAME: SN-9 Wasp

WEAPON TYPE: Revolver

ACTION: Auto-rotating barrel

AMMUNITION: 9 millimeter hypervelocity sabot rounds

RATE OF FIRE: 4 rounds per second

SELECTIVE FIRE: One shot, two burst, empty magazine, safety

MAGAZINE CAPACITY: 6 rounds

EXTRAS: Detachable light and scope with IR and movement sensing. Gyroscopic-stabilized aiming system accurate to 135 meters.

LENGTH: 228 millimeters

WEIGHT: 1.1 kilograms

This gun is often acquired privately by soldiers when standard issue sidearms are not sufficient for many of the operations. The SN-9 Wasp has the reliability of a revolver and the necessary punch to make sure the enemy goes down when hit. It is of particular use on Pandora, where many of the dangerous animals (and aboriginals) are large and cannot be always be brought down with standard RDA-issued sidearms.

The position of the firing chamber behind the center of gravity allows the barrel to be centered over the handgrip, which improves the pistol's balance.

CARB Weapon System

Manufacturer: Matanza Arms Corp.

The Cellular Ammunition Rifle Base (CARB) weapon system is an advanced, modular small-arms system designed to fit the needs of modern infantry as well as private military units and security personnel. The system is built around the CARB base unit, which is a fully automatic assault rifle with a bullpup configuration. A variety of modular equipment can be attached quickly and easily to the base unit.

Matanza Arms Corp. developed the system to streamline their infantry weapons array down to a single multifunctional system. Although never adopted as the primary weapon system by any of the world's major armies, it became widely popular with private military contractors (PMCs) and various special forces throughout Earth. Valued for its adaptability, simplicity, reliability, and innovative ammunition capacities, it quickly earned respect from these groups. The system has seen action on almost all continents and also on numerous off-world locations.

CARB Base Unit

Use on Pandora: Both "inside the wire" defensive use and "outside the wire" escort and patrol use. All-around workhorse.

Manufacturer: Matanza Arms Corp.

Weapon Type: Automatic rifle

Action: Gas-operated, revolving breech

Ammunition: 6.2 x 35

Rate of Fire: 600 rounds per minute

Selective Fire: Safety, semiautomatic, fully automatic

Magazine Capacity: 80 rounds in a disposable plastic box magazine with built-in ammo counter

Length: 390 millimeters

Weight: 2.54 kilograms empty, 3 kilograms loaded

Bullpup configuration (action and magazine both behind trigger), allows for an increase in the relative length of the barrel and thus more lethality at a distance. Base model can be modified with extended barrel, 20-millimeter munition launcher, day/night stabilized optical zoom scope. Ammo for munition launcher can include high explosives that are fin-stabilized, also grenade and tactical buckshot. Programmable airburst capability.

CARB Shotgun

USE ON PANDORA: Force multiplier during security missions

MANUFACTURER: Matanza Arms Corp.

ACTION: Gas-operated (optional pump action with extended barrel section)

AMMUNITION: 20-millimeter shells

MAGAZINE CAPACITY: 20 rounds in disposable plastic box magazine with built-in ammo counter

CAPABILITIES: Programmable air burst, CARB 20-millimeter munition launcher base, extended barrel, carry handle, scope, torch/fore-grip unit, recoil absorbing stock

LENGTH: 810 millimeters

WEIGHT: 5.2 kilograms empty, 6 kilograms loaded

SCOPE: Omnisight Optics, reflex sight, red-dot sight, built-in laser, head-up display

Used as a backstop defensive measure and for capacity layering during security missions. This weapon can utilize a wide array of 20-millimeter munitions such as air-burst grenades, high-explosive rounds, armor-penetrating rounds, fléchette rounds (metal darts), cluster munitions delivery, etc.

GS-221 .30 Caliber Light Machine Gun

USE ON PANDORA: Door gun for Samson Tiltrotor, squad support

MANUFACTURER: IBSF Protection Solutions

WEAPON TYPE: Light machine gun

ACTION: Gas-operated, closed-bolt

AMMUNITION: 7.62 WHTO (.30 caliber)/various types (FMJ, armor-piercing, tracer, etc.)

RATE OF FIRE: 700 rounds per minute

SELECTIVE FIRE: Safety, semiautomatic, full automatic

MAGAZINE CAPACITY: Barrel magazine contains one hundred rounds

DRY WEIGHT: 11.79 kilograms (without ammo can)

LENGTH: 1346 millimeters

The GS-221 is manufactured by IBSF Protection Solutions, a multinational arms and ammunition dealer located in Stuttgart, Germany. The company was originally only an ammunition and tactical gear manufacturer called Protection Solutions, but later changed its name in support of its highly successful namesake technology, IBSF (Imprint Ballistics Solution on Firing).

MBS-9M .50 Caliber Hydra

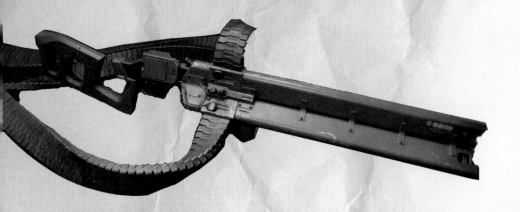

Use on Pandora: Door gun for transport on gunship

Manufacturer: Masa-Cirre Ltd., Modular Belt Systems Divisions

Weapon Type: Heavy suppression and clearance

Configuration: Tri-barrel arrangement. Stock with spade handle grips. Can be mounted with aircraft remote body fixture.

Ammunition: Gauss media: 50-millimeter uranium needle rounds, tracer rounds

Rate of Fire: 600, 1200, or 1800 rounds per minute automatic

Selective Fire: Automatic

Inbuilt Scope: Multifunction viewfinder, thermal/night/movement. A/V output to external monitor. 80x optical zoom.

Dry Weight: 14 kilograms (without ammo can)

Length: 1473 millimeters

The MBS-9M's primary function on Pandora has been as a Samson Tilt-rotor and Scorpion Gunship door gun. The gun allows the operator a manual firing configuration, with ammunition supplied by the over-all Samson vehicle weapons platform through the use of Masa-Cirre's proprietary Modular Belt System technology (MBS). In this way the crew chief has an overview of all weapons systems aboard the aircraft and can assess situations accordingly in real-time.

The MBS-9M is a manual single-operator support weapon version of the Masa-Cirre MBS automated weapon system. It is the smallest variant in the MBS system, and unlike its automated and remote-operated brothers, it is designed for adaptability and configurability for use by ground forces; it can be held like a rifle or light machine gun, or mounted for gunners on vehicles and aircraft as needed. It is a modular weapon system, meaning it has various components that can be configured for different firing missions.

SCALE: PANDORAN CREATURES AND RDA EQUIPMENT

RESOURCES DEVELOPMENT ADMINISTRATION

RDA RECRUITMENT HOLOPOSTS ARE
FICTION. WORK CONDITIONS FOR MINERS ON
PANDORA ARE DEPLORABLE, DANGEROUS.
THOSE MINERS LUCKY ENOUGH TO MAKE IT
BACK TO EARTH USUALLY SUFFER LONG-
TERM HEALTH PROBLEMS, INCLUDING
BLOOD AND BONE CANCERS, EARLY-
ONSET ALZHEIMER'S, AND CLINICAL
DEPRESSION. MOST BECOME ESTRANGED
FROM FAMILIES, FRIENDS, AND END UP AS
LARGELY DYSFUNCTIONAL MEMBERS OF
SOCIETY. HEFTY BONUSES ARE USUALLY
EATEN UP BY MEDICAL BILLS.
    THESE RDA TRANSMISSIOS REGARDING
OPERATIONS ON PANDORA WERE
INTERCEPTED LAST YEAR.

ESM 01 UPDATE (EYES ONLY)

Mining operations at ESM 01 (the main mine on Pandora) have proceeded according to plan, despite casualty rates running somewhat higher than anticipated. Continuing reports of miners feeling strange tactile sensations and distortions in vision and hearing—likely the result of electromagnetic field. Some report disturbing thoughts or compulsions, irregular heartbeats, limb paralysis, muscle tremors, or vertigo and nausea.

Excavation has been carried out with standard nonferrous beryllium copper and tungsten carbide fusion-electric powered mining equipment modified with sealed operator cockpits and atmosphere filtration units.

A typical mining cycle involves placing chemical charges above an ore deposit using satellite-positioned drill trucks, detonating the charges to loosen the overburden, then removing the overburden with excavators and dozers. After the ore has been exposed it is carefully removed with diggers and trucks; if the ore is pure enough to spontaneously levitate, special belt diggers feeding into covered trucks are used instead.

The mine and refinery complex is relatively untroubled by Pandoran life-forms, with automatic cannons on guard towers easily able to cope with marauding ground and air attackers. Regular effluent sprays around the perimeter of the complex keep vegetation in check.

Vehicle cabs are shielded against toxins, but mining personnel are advised not to spend more than twenty minutes per day outside their vehicle cabs and are routinely decontaminated before they are allowed into Hell's Gate.

The mine pits are terraced to allow easy access for vehicles, and are graduated outward. The shape and size of the known deposits at ESM 01 are such that over the mine's anticipated thirty-year lifetime the three excavation pits will eventually merge into a single crater about 4 kilometers across.

HELL'S GATE

RDA ESC 01
RE: Update on Construction
Sent via McKinney

Construction of Hell's Gate is nearing its final stages. A pentagonal perimeter fence (each side 1.89 kilometers long) encloses 6.16 square kilometers. Major weapons towers at each apex provide heavy munitions defense against surface and air intrusions by large hostile Pandoran wildlife, while four smaller towers spaced 250 meters apart along each side handle intrusions by smaller life-forms, including burrowing attacks. A cleared strip 30 meters wide surrounds the base, regularly patrolled by automatic plant-clearing machinery that keeps the jungle at bay through regular administration of acidic mining by-products.

Slightly more than a third of the site is taken up by the shuttle runway, VTOL pads, and associated support facilities; a similar area is occupied by vehicle storage, the armor vault, and a light industrial plant mainly used to fabricate parts for mining equipment and ammunition for base defense.

Administrative structures, a barracks for Sec-Ops staff, studio-style apartments for technicians and mine workers, and an airtight condominium for senior staff occupy the remainder of Hell's Gate.

Protein and carbohydrate synthesis using Pandoran vegetive matter continues to meet nutritional needs of all RDA staff. Improvement in microfilters has led to marked reduction in cases of amoebic dysentery and necrotizing ulcerative gingivitis.

Recreational facilities such as the base commissary (popularly known as Hell's Kitchen) are shared, except for an unpressurized section between the research labs and the landing zone mainly used by members of the avatar program for athletic training and field sports.

GLOSSARY

AILERONS. Hinged control surfaces on the back of a wing, including those on the Valkyrie shuttle. Used to control lateral balance of the craft.

AMNIO TANK. Large tank used to grow genetically engineered avatar bodies during flight from Earth to Pandora. Similar devices are widely used on Earth for organ regeneration.

APEX PREDATOR. A predator, such as the thanator or great leonopteryx, that is at the top of the food chain in its area and is not preyed upon by other creatures.

ARBOREAL. Referring to a creature who lives and feeds in trees, such as the prolemuris.

AURORAL. Referring to the brilliant displays of light that appear in the upper atmosphere, usually near polar regions. Caused by the excitation of atoms due to magnetic fields. Because of Pandora's intense magnetic fields, auroral displays are more dramatic than on Earth.

BIOFUELS. Any fuel derived from processed living matter, usually vegetive.

BIOME. A region of distinct flora and fauna, such as the rainforests of Pandora.

BIOREMEDIATION. The use of plants, fungi, or microorganisms to restore an environment to a cleaner, more natural condition. Many of the plants on Pandora have the ability to absorb toxins, which could have implications on Earth.

BIOTA. The flora and fauna within a specific region or time period: the biota of the floating mountains or the biota of the Jurassic period.

CANOPY. Upper layer of forest, usually the tops of trees.

CHITINOUS. Referring to chitin, a very hard long-chain organic polymer found in the walls of fungi, exoskeletons, and beaks. Many Pandoran creatures have chitinous formations that are used as natural armor.

CONTINENTAL DRIFT. The movement of continents over geologic time. The term is something of a misnomer, since it refers to the now-discounted belief that continents "drifted" over the Earth's liquid core. The theory has now been replaced with confirmed studies of plate tectonics, although the term "continental drift" is still widely used to describe the movement of continents. Because of various natural forces, Pandora has a much higher rate of continental drift.

DELTA WINGS. Aircraft wings, such as those on the Valkyrie shuttle, which have a triangular shape when viewed from above.

ELECTROCYTES. Organic cells used by animals, including the medusa, to generate and transfer electricity and electrical signals. The cells are positively charged on one side, and negatively charged on the other.

EPIPHYTE. A plant that grows on top of another plant as structural support. They are not parasitic. Often found in rainforest canopies.

EYWA. Guiding force and deity of Pandora and the Na'vi. Sometimes scientists hypothesize that all living things on Pandora connect to Eywa through a system of neuro-conductive antenna. Some believe interconnectedness, which on Earth is often considered a spiritual concept, exists in a physical and tangible way on Pandora. The Na'vi believe that Eywa, in turn, acts to keep the ecosystems of Pandora in perfect balance.

FERROMAGNETIC. A material that is susceptible to magnetic fields and magnetization. Because of Pandoran magnetic fields, mining equipment must be made of exotic and expensive nonferromagnetic material.

GLOTTAL STOP. A consonant sound created when vocal cords are constricted and released, as when saying "uh-oh." Used both by the Na'vi on Pandora (mostly in song) and various aboriginal Earth races.

HYDROGEN SULFIDE. A colorless, toxic gas present in the Pandoran atmosphere. One of several gases that necessitate the use of an exopack by human colonists.

LAGRANGIAN POINTS. A point in space at which there is a balance between the gravitational forces of two larger bodies and the orbital motion of a third smaller body.

LOU GEHRIG'S DISEASE. Amytrophic lateral sclerosis—a progressive neurological disease named after a famed baseball player of the early twentieth century. The disease is caused by the degeneration of motor neurons. Stephen Hawking, the famed twenty-first-century physicist, suffered from the disease. Several toxic plants on Pandora, including the cycad, contain a poison that can cause symptoms similar to the disease.

MAGNETIC FLUX LINES. Lines of a magnetic field that emanate from a magnetized object.

MAGNETIC FLUX TUBE. A tube-shaped area of space that contains a magnetic field that is more powerful than surrounding areas. Common around stars, including our own sun, especially in areas of sunspots. In some conditions, a flux tube can form between Pandora and Polyphemus, creating a powerful electrical current between the two bodies and resultant lightning storms.

MICROTONAL. Referring to music that uses intervals smaller than those between the twelve notes of traditional Western music.

NACELLES. A cover that houses engines, fuel, or equipment on an aircraft.

NEOLITHIC: Stage in human development in the later part of Stone Age when use of polished, ground weapons became prevalent. Na'vi are said to live in a Neolithic society, although in many ways they are much further advanced than the human precedent.

OFFAL. Internal organs of animals, sometimes used as a food source but often discarded. Related to the word "awful."

OVERBURDEN. In mining, the (soil, rock, mud, etc., that covers the material to be mined.

PANGAEA. Geologists theorize that some 250 million years ago, one supercontinent existed and later broke up to form the existing continents. The lan mass was named Pangaea by Alfred Wegener, the scientist who developed the theory of continental drift.

PERMALLOY. Specifically, an alloy comprised of nickel and iron. But the term has come to refer to a wide class of superstrength, lightweight composite alloys that can resist magnetic fields. Used in aircraft and spacecraft because of their properties.

PEYOTE SONGS. A form of musical ritual performed by Native Americans of the Southwest. Sung in conjunction with the ritual use of peyote, a cactus that contains psychoactive alkaloids. Peyote rituals are similar to the Uniltaron ceremony of the Na'vi on Pandora.

PLANIMAL. Colloquial term for zooplantae, or hybrid life-form that has characteristics of both plant and animal.

POLYGYNY. Mating structure in which the male has two or more female mates.

POSITIVE FEEDBACK. The amplification of a force or effect, e.g., when one wave magnifies another's force.

PREHENSILE. Description of a tail that is able to grasp, such as that of the prolemuris or the Na'vi.

PSIONIC LINK OR "PSILINK." Array of devices used to project cognitive commands into external biological unit. Used to project consciousness of avatar operator into avatar body.

PSYCHOACTIVE. A drug or substance that acts upon the central nervous system, either to change mood and behavior or to create hallucinations. Several creatures on Pandora, including the arachnoid, contain psychoactive venom.

RIVER BLINDNESS (ONCHOCERCIASIS). An infectious form of blindness transmitted through the bite of a black fly and caused by a nematode that can live for up to fifteen years in the human body. A hundred million people are infected with this parasite.

SCATOLOGY. The study of animal feces to provide information on diet, range, and overall health.

SITE 26. Small, remote outpost on one of the floating mountains. Contains psilink unit.

TREE OF SOULS. Found near Hometree, it is one of the Na'vi most sacred sites. The Na'vi believe it is the strongest manifestation of Ewya on Pandora.

TREE OF VOICES. Willowlike tree that the Na'vi believe allows the Omaticaya to commune with both their ancestors and Eywa by entwining their queues with the roots of the tree.

UNGULATES. Name means "hoofed animal." Term refers to groups of mammals, such as zebra, donkeys, and horses. Several species on Pandora, including the hammerhead titanothere, have been found to have features, including chewing habits, that are similar to Terran ungulates.

UNILTARON. Na'vi ceremony in which a prospective warrior ingests psychoactive agents. Subsequent hallucinations are believed to be revelatory by Na'vi. Similar to mescaline ceremonies of Native Americans of the Southwest.

VACUOLE. Membrane in cells of plants and fungi that create enclosed compartments serving a variety of functions, including storage of liquid or sequestration of toxins.

VULCANISM. The presence of volcanic activity in a region. Pandora has a pronounced degree of vulcanism that has increased the density of the atmosphere.

VTOL. Abbreviation for vertical takeoff and landing. Includes helicopters and some fixed-wing aircraft.

WOODSPRITE. A small, floating seedpod from the willowlike "sacred tree." The Na'vi believe that woodsprites are portents or "signs" from Eywa. Known as *atokirina* by the Na'vi.

XENOBOTANY. The study of plant life on planets other than Earth. Until the discovery of Pandora, this was largely a theoretical subject, but it is now at the forefront of science.

XENOMUSICOLOGISTS. Musicologists who study the music of off-Earth cultures. The field was largely theoretical until the discovery of the Na'vi. Funding for this once-esoteric subject sky-rocketed with discovery of Na'vi. Also referred to as "astromusicologists."

XENON. A colorless, odorless gas that is found in trace elements in Earth's atmosphere. In the twenty-first century, it was used in lamps and as a general anesthetic. With its higher concentrations on Pandora, xenon becomes toxic.

YUCATAN ASTEROID STRIKE. Catastrophic asteroid impact sixty-five million years ago that is believed to have caused mass extinctions and formed Mexico's Chicxulub Basin near the Yucatan peninsula. Some xenobotanists theorize that biological material was shot into space and migrated to Pandora.

ZOOPLANTAE. Hybrid life-form that has characteristics of both plant and animal, including a nervous system more animal-like than plantlike.

NA'VI-ENGLISH DICTIONARY

NA'VI	ENGLISH
'ampi	touch
'aw	one
'awkx	cliff
'awpo	one individual
'aws<u>iteng</u>	together
'awve	first
'<u>e</u>'al	worst
'<u>e</u>ko	attack
'<u>e</u>kong	beat (rhythmic)
'<u>e</u>ngeng	level
'<u>e</u>veng	child
'<u>e</u>vi	kid (affectionate form of "child")
'i'awn	remain, stay
'iheyu	spiral
'Ìnglìsì	English language
'<u>i</u>t	bit, small amount
'itan	son
'ite	daughter
'ok	remembrance
'ong	unfold, blossom

'upe	what (thing)
'upxare	message
a	which, that
äie	vision
alaksì	ready
alìm	far away, at a distance
Amhul	child's name
Änsìt	child's name
apxa	large
atan	light
atokirina'	atokirina, seeds of the great tree
ätxäle	request
atxkxe	land
au	drum (made of skin)
aungia	sign, omen
ayfo (ayfo)	they
aylaru	to the others (contraction of *aylaheru*)
aynga	you
ayoe	we (exclusive)
ayoeng	we (inclusive)
ean	blue
eltu	brain
eltu si	pay attention, quit goofing off
eltungawng	brainworm
emza'u	pass (a test)
eo	before, in front of
eyk	lead
eyktan	leader
Eywa	Eywa PN
Eywa ngahu	good-bye, Eywa (be with you)
fa	with (by means of)
faheu	smell
fi'u	this (thing)
fifya	this way, like this
fikem	this (action)

fìpo	this one (person or thing)
fìtseng(e)	here, this place
fkarut	peel
fkeu	mighty
fko	one
fmawn	news, something to report
fmetok	test
fmi	try
fnu	quiet (= be quiet)
fo	they
fpak	hold off, suspend action
fpe'	send
fpeio	challenge (ceremonial)
fpi	for the sake of
fpom	well-being; peace
fpxafaw	medusa (animal)
fpxäkìm	enter
fra'u	everything
frapo	everyone
ftang	stop
fte	so that
fteke	so that not, lest
ftia	study
ftu	from (direction)
ftue	easy
ftxey	choose
fu	or
fya'o	path, way
fyape	how
fyawìntxu	guide
ha	So (or "in that case")
hapxì	part
hasey	done, finished
hawnu	protect, shelter
hì'i	small
hiyìk	funny (strange)
hrrap	danger

hu	with (accompaniment)
hufwe	wind
hum	leave, depart
i'en	stringed instrument
Iknimaya	Stairway to Heaven
ikran	ikran, mountain banshee
ilä (also: ìlä)	by, via, following
ioang	animal, beast
irayo	thank you
ka	across
kä	go
kaltxì	hello
kämakto	ride out
kame	see (spiritual sense)
kangay	valid
karyu	teacher
kato	rhythm
kawkrr	never
kawng	bad, evil
kawtu	no one
ke	not
ke'u	nothing
kea	no (before a noun)
kehe	no
kelku	home
kelku si	live, dwell
Kelutral	Hometree
kempe	what (action)
kenong	model, represent, exemplify
kerusey	dead
ketuwong	alien
kewong	alien
keye'ung	insanity
ki'ong	kind of fruit or vegetable
kifkey	world (physical, solid)
kìm	spin
kin	need

kinä	seven
kinam	leg
kinamtil	knee
kìng	thread
kip	among
kìte'e	service
kiyevame	good-bye, see you again soon
kllfrivo'	be responsible
kllkulat	dig up
kllkxem	stand
kllpxìltu	territory
kllte	ground
krr	time
krrnekx	take/consume time
krrpe	when
kunsìp	gunship
kurakx	drive out
kxam	middle, midpoint
kxamtseng	center (or place in the middle)
kxangangang	boom
kxanì	forbidden
kxawm	perhaps, maybe
kxener	kind of fruit or vegetable
kxetse	tail
lahe	other
lam	seem, appear
lapo	other one (person or thing)
latem	change
law	clear, certain
lehrrap	dangerous
lertu	colleague
lì'u	word
lok	close to
lonu	release, let go
lrrtok	smile
lu	be (am, is, are)
lumpe	why

makto	ride
mawey	calm
me<u>f</u>o	they (those two)
me<u>n</u>ari	eyes (two)
me<u>u</u>ia	honor
meyp	weak
mì	in
<u>mik</u>yun	ear
mìn	turn
mìso	away (position)
m<u>llte</u>	agree
moe	we two (exclusive)
mokri	voice
muiä	proper, fair, right
mun'<u>i</u>	cut
<u>mu</u>ne	two
<u>mu</u>nge	take, bring
muntxa	mated
na	like, as
<u>na</u>'rìng	forest
Na'vi	Na'vi; the people
nang	particle for surprise or exclamation
<u>nan</u>tang	viperwolf
<u>n</u>ari	eye
nari si	watch out, be careful
nawm	great, noble
ne	to (direction)
ne <u>kll</u>te!	get down! (literally, "to the ground!")
ne'<u>ìm</u>	back (direction)
nekx	burn, consume
neto	away (direction)
neu	want
nga	you
ngawng	worm
ngay	true
ngenga	you (honorific form)
ngop	create
nì'aw	only

nì'**awtu**	alone (as one person)
nì'**awve**	first
nì'it	small amount, a bit
nì'ul	more
niä	grab
Nìayoeg	like us
(pronounced nay**weng**)	
nìftue	easily
nìftxavang	passionately, with all heart
nìhawng	too, excessively
nìltsan	well
nìmun	again
nìn	look at
nìngay	truly
nìtam	enough
nìtut	continually
nìtxan	much
nìwin	fast
nìwotx	all (of), in toto, completely
nulkrr	longer (time)
nume	learn
oe	I
oeng	we two (you and I)
ohe	I (deferential or ceremonial form)
olo'	clan
olo'eyktan	clan leader
Omatikaya	Omaticaya
omum	know
ontu	nose
pähem	arrive
pak	particle for disparagement
palulukan	thanator
pam	sound
pamtseo	music
pänutìng	promise (a thing to someone)
pätsì	badge
pawm	ask

pe	what (before a noun)
pefya	how
pehem	what (action)
pehrr	when
pelun	why
peng	tell
peseng	where
pesu	who
peu	what (thing)
pey	wait
pizayu	ancestor
plltxe	speak
po	he, she
poan	he
poe	she
pongu	group of people, party
pxan	worthy
pxasul	fresh, appealing as food
pxay	many
pxel	like, as
pxi	sharp
pxun	arm
pxuntil	elbow
rä'ä	do not
ral	meaning
ralpeng	interpret
Ralu	child's name
rawke	alarm cry
renu	pattern
rey	live
rikx	move, shift position
rim	yellow
rina'	seed
riti	stingbat
rol	sing
ronsem	mind
rutxe	please

sa'nok	mother
san	saying; quote
sa'nu	mommy
sänume	teaching, instruction
sat	that (after *ftu* only)
sempu	daddy
sempul	father
set	now
sevin	pretty
seyri	lip
seze	blue flower
si	do, make
sì	and
sìk	unquote
sìlronsem	clever (thing)
sìltsan	good
ska'a	destroy
skxawng	moron
slä	but
slu	become
sngä'i	begin, start
sngä'ikrr	beginning, start time
snumìna	dim (of a person)
som	hot
spe'e	capture
spe'etu	captive
srak(e)	marker for yes-no questions
srane	yes
sreu	dance
srung	help, assistance
steftxaw	examine
stum	almost
sutx	track, lock up
swaw	moment
swirä	creature
swizaw	arrow
swok	sacred
swotu	sacred place
syaw	call

ta	from (various uses)
ta'em	from above
täftxu	weave
täftxuyu	weaver
takuk	strike
talioang	sturmbeest
tam	suffice, "do"
tangek	trunk (of a tree)
tanhì	star
taron	hunt
taronyu	hunter
taw	sky
tawng	dive
tawng	duck
Tawtute	Sky Person
te	particle used in full names
telem	cord
tengfya	as (= same way as)
tengkrr	while (= same time as)
terkup	die
teswotìng	grant
teya	full
teylu	beetle larva(e)
tìfmetok	test
tìftang	stopping
tìhawnu	protection
tìkawng	evil
tìkenong	example
tìkin	need
til	joint, hinge
tìng	give
tìng mikyun	listen
(usually pronounced: tìm mikyun)	
tìng nari	look
(usually pronounced: tìn nari)	
tìngay	truth
tìran	walk
tirea	spirit
tireafya'o	spirit path

tìreaioang	spirit animal
tìrey	life
tìrol	song
tìtxur	strength
to	than; comparative marke
tok	be at, occupy a space
toktor	doctor
tokx	body
tompa	rain
toruk	great leonopteryx
trr	day
tsa'u	that (thing)
Tsahaylu	bond (neural connection)
Tsahìk	Tsahik, matriarch
tsakem	that (action)
tsakrr	then, at that time
tsam	war
tsampongu	war party
tsamsiyu	warrior
tsap'alute	apology
tsat	that (as object)
tsatseng	there, that place
tsatu	that person
tsawke	sun
tsawl	big (in stature)
tse'a	see (physical sense)
tseng(e)	place
tsengpe	where
tseo	art
tsìng	four
tsìvol	thirty-two (octal: 40)
tsko	bow (weapon)
tsko swizaw	bow and arrow
tskxe	rock, stone
tskxekeng	training, exercise
tslam	understand
tsleng	false
tslolam	Got it. I understand.
tsmuk, tsmuktu	sibling

tsmukan	brother
tsmuke	sister
tsnì	that
tspang	kill
tsranten	matter, be of import
tsteu	brave
tsun	can, be able
tswayon	fly
tsyal	wing
tuk<u>ru</u>	spear
tul	run
tung	allow
<u>tu</u>pe	who
<u>tu</u>te	person
tute<u>an</u>	male (person)
tute<u>e</u>	female (person)
txan	great (in quantity); much
<u>txantslusam</u>	wise, much-knowing
txe'<u>lan</u>	heart
txele	matter (subject)
txen	awake
txep	fire
txey	halt
txìm	butt, rear end
txìng	leave, abandon
txo	if
txoa	forgiveness
<u>txo</u>kefyaw	if not, or else
txon	night
txopu	fear
txum	poison
txur	strong
<u>u</u>lte	and
ultxa	meeting
<u>u</u>nil	dream
<u>U</u>niltaron	Dream Hunt
uniltìrantokx	avatar; dreamwalker body
uniltìranyu	dreamwalker

utral	tree
Utral Aymokriyä	Tree of Voices
virä	spread, proliferate
virä	spread, proliferate
vofu	sixteen
vrrtep	demon
vul	branch (of a tree)
way	song
waytelem	songchord
wìntxu	show
wrrpa	outside
wutso	dinner, served meal
ye'rìn	soon
yerik	hexapede
yey	straight
yìm	bind
yol	long (of time)
yom	eat
yomtìng	feed
yur	wash
za'ärìp	pull
za'u	come
zamunge	bring
zekwä	finger
zene	must
zìsìt	year
zong	save
zongtseng	safe place, refuge
zoplo	offense, insult

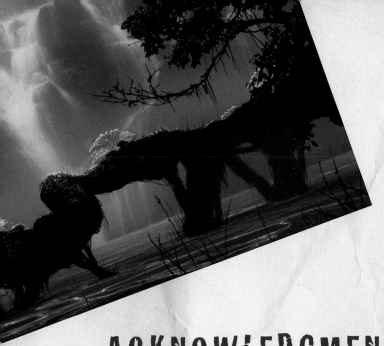

ACKNOWLEDGMENTS

This book is the result of the collaboration between an esteemed group of scientists, academics, and writers who brought their expertise and vision to the world of James Cameron's *Avatar*. The book would not have been possible without the contributions of the following: Stephen Ballantyne, Wanda Bryant, Randall Frakes, Paul Frommer, Jodie Holt, James Tanenbaum, and Richard Taylor.

Unending thanks go to *Avatar* producer Jon Landau for his help and support. And, of course, to James Cameron, who created the remarkable world of Pandora and allowed us to visit.

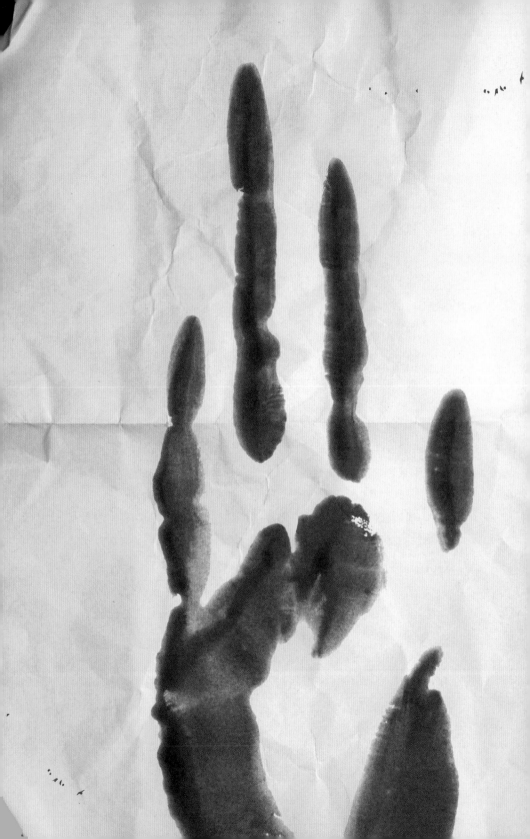